FASTLANE F₹EEDOM
"ENHANCING LIVES OF MILLIONS"

A Product of Fastlane Freedom with Vision of
Enhancing Lives of Millions

Parenting Essentials

Vinod Singh

"Connect the Vision"
Nexus Stories Publication
Bharata

NEXUS STORIES PUBLICATION®
Surat, Gujarat, India.

Title – Parenting Essentials
First Published by Nexus Stories Publication 2025

ISBN # 978-93-48504-08-1

Author: Vinod Singh
Email: fastlanefreedom7@gmail.com

Publication

Nexus Stories Publication®, Surat (Gujarat), Bhārata
www.nexus-stories.com # +91 87800 80718

Preface

Ah, the beautiful, bewildering journey of parenting! It's a path paved with tiny handprints, echoing laughter, and the occasional tear-stained frustration. We pour our hearts and souls into these little beings, nurturing their dreams while navigating the labyrinth of their ever-evolving needs. Yet, amidst the overwhelming love and fierce protectiveness, we often find ourselves questioning our steps, yearning for a guiding light in the sometimes-murky waters of raising the next generation. What if there was a voice, forged in the fires of entrepreneurial success and tempered with the wisdom of fatherhood, offering a fresh perspective? Vinod Singh, the visionary behind Fastlane Freedom, understands the relentless drive for achievement. But what happens when that drive intersects with the profound responsibility of raising children? His book promises to be more than just another parenting guide; it's a heartfelt conversation, a beacon of clarity, offering solace and strategies for weaving success in both your professional and personal life, ensuring you thrive alongside your children. Get ready to embark on a transformative journey, one that honors both your ambitions and the precious souls entrusted to your care.

- KB Joshi (Director, Nexus Stories Publication)

Profile

About Us

Fastlane Freedom was launched in 2019 by Vinod Singh, a Belief Changer, following 3.5 years of research on mindfulness and its relationship to money. Fastlane Freedom is motivated by a vision of **'Enhancing Millions'** by transforming people's mindsets to improve their financial conditions. Vinod has 16 years of professional experience and is dedicated to offering high-quality, practical content on Mindfulness, Money, Business, Parenting, and Student Life.

Countless people throughout the world suffer as a result of incorrect ideas that add stress to their financial, personal, professional, commercial, and social life. To address this, we provide insights based on scientific data, real-life case studies, and our own knowledge.

Profile of Mr. Vinod Singh

Essentially, he comes from a farming background. After finishing his engineering degree (B. Tech, Mechanical), he has started his career and worked from well-known MNCs.

He has been studying "How Beliefs Affect Our Life, Especially Financial Life" for almost 7 years. The study began with the question, "Why are some people financially successful for generations while others are not?"

He launched his blogging website, www.fastlanefreedom.com, in January 2021. This website contains informative and life-changing posts (now over 1000) on themes such as mindfulness, money, business growth, parenting, student life, and popular quotes.

As a serial entrepreneur, till now he has covered thousands of Peoples /Students /Businessmen / Professions and also connected with several MSME & Corporate groups.

Scan the QR code to connect with his profile.

*****

Index

1. Attachment Theory: The Science of Emotional Bonds

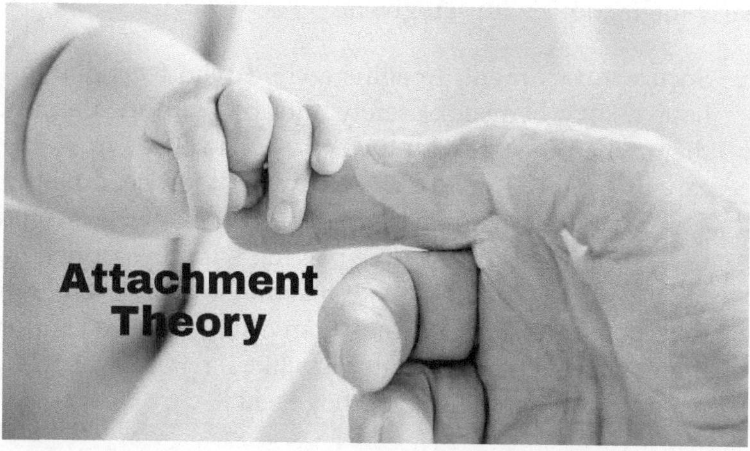

Attachment theory, made by a psychologist named John Bowlby in the 1950s, helps us understand how people connect with each other. It looks at the special bonds' kids form with the people who take care of them, like parents or guardians. These early bonds affect how we feel and act even when we grow up. This theory says that how good these early bonds are, whether they make us feel safe or not, really shapes how we see ourselves, others, and the world. By learning about the four main types of attachment and how they affect our relationships and feelings, we can see how important it is to have caring experiences when we're young. Understanding attachment theory helps us know ourselves better, understand others more deeply, and build stronger relationships in our lives.

> *"Our early relationships provide the scaffolding for our emotional well-being throughout life."* – **Daniel J. Siegel**

- **The Four Attachment Styles**

According to attachment theory, there are four main attachment styles that individuals develop based on their early interactions with caregivers:

1. **Secure Attachment**: Imagine a child who feels like they have a cozy blanket of safety and love wrapped around them when they're with their caregivers. They trust their caregivers to be there for them when they need help or comfort. This trust makes them feel confident to explore the world around them, like playing with toys or making new friends. They know that if something goes wrong or they get scared, their caregivers will be there to comfort them and make things better. It's like having a warm hug waiting for them whenever they need it.

2. **Anxious-Preoccupied Attachment**: Think of someone who feels like they're always walking on a tightrope in their relationships, afraid of falling off. They worry a lot about whether their loved ones truly care about them and fear being left alone. To ease this fear, they constantly seek reassurance from their partners or friends, asking for proof that they are loved and wanted. They might cling to their loved ones tightly, afraid that if they let go, they'll be abandoned. It's like needing someone to hold their hand constantly to feel safe.

3. **Dismissive-Avoidant Attachment**: Picture a person who prefers to keep an emotional distance from others, like they're surrounded by an invisible bubble. They value their independence highly and don't like depending on others for support or comfort. They might find it hard to express their feelings openly and tend to keep things to themselves. They prefer to deal with problems alone and might seem distant or detached in their relationships. It's like building a protective wall around themselves to keep others from getting too close.

4. **Fearful-Avoidant Attachment**: Imagine someone caught in a tug-of-war between their desire for closeness and their fear of getting hurt. They crave intimacy and connection with others but are also afraid of getting too close and being vulnerable. This internal conflict can lead to relationships that feel chaotic and unpredictable, like a rollercoaster ride of emotions. They might push people away one moment and then pull them close the next, unsure of what they truly want or need. It's like wanting to hug someone tightly but also feeling scared to do so at the same time.

- **The Role of Caregiver Responsiveness**

The role of caregiver responsiveness in attachment theory is crucial in shaping a child's emotional development. Caregiver responsiveness refers to how attentively and effectively caregivers meet the needs of their child. When caregivers promptly and sensitively respond to a child's cues for comfort and support, it fosters a deep sense of security and trust within the child. This responsive care creates a nurturing environment where the child feels understood, valued, and loved, laying the foundation for what psychologists term a secure attachment. In these secure attachments, children feel confident in their caregivers' availability and support, enabling them to explore their environment and develop a healthy sense of autonomy.

Conversely, when caregivers are inconsistent or unresponsive to a child's needs, it can have detrimental effects on the child's emotional well-being. Without the consistent presence and support of responsive caregivers, children may experience feelings of uncertainty, anxiety, and even fear. This lack of reliable support can lead to the formation of insecure attachment patterns. In such patterns, children may struggle to trust others or feel safe in relationships, as they have not developed a strong sense of security in their primary caregivers. These insecure attachment patterns can persist into adulthood, influencing how individuals form and maintain relationships, as well as their overall mental health and well-being. Therefore, caregiver responsiveness plays a critical role in shaping the attachment bonds that profoundly impact a child's emotional and social development.

- Impact on Relationships and Mental Health

The attachment style we form during childhood can profoundly shape our adult relationships and mental well-being. Those who experienced secure attachments in childhood typically navigate adult relationships with greater ease. They tend to have healthier bonds, feeling secure in themselves and their connections with others. They possess the emotional skills to manage stress and express their feelings effectively. Conversely, individuals who developed insecure attachments in childhood may encounter challenges in forming and maintaining relationships in adulthood. Their early experiences may lead to difficulties trusting others and establishing intimacy, which can strain interpersonal connections. This struggle to connect can contribute to feelings of anxiety, loneliness, or depression, impacting their overall mental health. Thus, the early patterns of attachment play a significant role in shaping not only our relationships but also our emotional well-being throughout life.

- **Applying Attachment Theory in Practice**

Understanding attachment theory can be valuable in various fields, including psychology, education, and parenting.

Therapy: Therapists use attachment theory to understand why people might struggle in their relationships or feel bad about themselves. They help their clients see how their early experiences with caregivers might be affecting them now. Then, they work together to develop new ways of thinking and behaving that can lead to healthier relationships and better self-esteem. For example, they might teach skills like communication or emotional regulation to help someone feel more secure and connected to others.

Teaching: Teachers can use attachment theory to create supportive and caring environments for their students. They understand that kids who feel safe and loved are more likely to learn and thrive. So, they might focus on building strong relationships with their students and providing a safe space where kids feel valued and understood.

Parenting: Parents play a huge role in shaping their child's attachment style. By learning about attachment theory, parents can understand the importance of responding to their child's needs with love and consistency. They can learn how to comfort their child when they're upset, and how to set boundaries in a loving way. This helps the child feel secure and loved, which lays the foundation for healthy relationships and good mental health later in life. So, applying attachment theory in parenting can lead to happier, healthier kids who grow into confident, caring adults.

Conclusion

In conclusion, attachment theory offers a profound lens through which to understand the intricacies of human relationships and emotional development. From the foundational bonds formed in early childhood to the complexities of adult connections, attachment styles play a pivotal role in shaping our behaviours, attitudes, and mental well-being. By recognizing the impact of caregiver responsiveness on attachment patterns and acknowledging the lasting effects of these patterns on our lives, we can strive to foster secure attachments and cultivate healthier, more fulfilling relationships. Embracing the principles of attachment theory not only enriches our understanding of ourselves and others but also empowers us to create nurturing environments where love, trust, and connection can flourish.

*****

2. The Role of Prenatal Learning in Early Childhood Development

Prenatal learning, the process by which fetuses begin to acquire knowledge and experience before birth, has been a topic of growing interest in developmental psychology and neuroscience. The concept challenges traditional views that learning begins postnatally and suggests that the foundations for early childhood development are laid down much earlier. This blog explores the mechanisms of prenatal learning, its impact on early childhood development, and the implications for parenting and educational practices.

"Prenatal learning is a testament to the remarkable adaptability and plasticity of the developing brain. By understanding and nurturing this early stage of development, we lay the groundwork for healthier and more resilient children." – Dr. Lise Eliot, *Neuroscientist and Author*

- **Understanding Prenatal Learning**

Prenatal learning involves the fetus's ability to perceive, process, and respond to sensory stimuli while still in the womb. Research indicates that fetuses can hear sounds, recognize voices, and even respond to musical rhythms. These early experiences are critical as they shape neural pathways and influence brain development. The fetal environment provides a rich tapestry of sensory inputs that the developing brain processes, laying the groundwork for postnatal learning and development. By engaging with the stimuli from the external world, the fetus begins to form the basis for cognitive functions, emotional regulation, and sensory integration that are crucial for later life stages.

- **Sensory Perception in the Womb**

By the end of the second trimester, the fetal sensory systems are sufficiently developed to start processing external stimuli. The auditory system, in particular, becomes functional around the 25th week of gestation. Fetuses can hear the mother's heartbeat, the flow of blood through the umbilical cord, and external sounds like music and voices. These auditory experiences are crucial for the development of the auditory cortex and can influence language acquisition and cognitive development postnatally. As the fetus hears the rhythm and melody of the mother's speech, it begins to familiarize itself with language patterns, which facilitates early language recognition and learning once born.

- **Mechanisms of Prenatal Learning**

The mechanisms underlying prenatal learning involve a complex interplay of genetic, epigenetic, and environmental factors. Key mechanisms include auditory learning, olfactory and taste learning, and tactile learning, each contributing uniquely to the developmental process.

- **Auditory Learning**

Studies have shown that fetuses can recognize and differentiate between sounds. Research by DeCasper and Spence (1986) demonstrated that newborns preferred their mother's voice over a stranger's voice, suggesting recognition based on prenatal exposure. Similarly, fetuses exposed to specific pieces of music showed a preference for those tunes after birth, indicating memory and learning capabilities. This auditory learning helps the fetus build neural connections that will be essential for language development and auditory processing skills. The ability to discern between different sounds and voices primes the brain for the complex task of language acquisition.

- **Olfactory and Taste Learning**

The fetus is also exposed to different tastes and smells through the amniotic fluid, which is influenced by the mother's diet. This exposure can shape the newborn's preferences and aversions. For instance, research indicates that babies exposed to garlic or anise in utero tend to show a preference for these flavours postnatally. This sensory learning occurs as molecules from the mother's diet pass into the amniotic fluid, allowing the fetus to sample a variety of flavours. This early exposure not only shapes taste preferences but also prepares the digestive system for processing a diverse range of foods after birth.

- **Tactile Learning**

Fetuses experience tactile stimuli through movements and the environment within the womb. These tactile experiences are believed to contribute to motor development and sensory integration. Studies have shown that fetuses exhibit habituation responses to repeated tactile stimuli, demonstrating an early form of learning and memory. Movements such as stretching, kicking, and touching the uterine wall help the fetus develop proprioception and body awareness. These tactile interactions are fundamental in developing the neural circuits that will later support motor skills and coordinated movements. Through these early tactile experiences, the fetus begins to understand its own body and its capabilities, setting the stage for postnatal motor development.

- **Impact on Early Childhood Development**

The experiences and learning that occur prenatally have profound implications for early childhood development, influencing cognitive, social, and emotional growth.

1. Cognitive Development

Prenatal auditory learning significantly impacts language development. Research shows that fetuses exposed to language patterns, rhythms, and specific sounds in the womb have a head start in language acquisition. This early exposure enhances phonetic discrimination abilities, which are crucial for later language learning. For instance, newborns can differentiate between the sounds of their native language and foreign languages, indicating early auditory processing and memory skills. Moreover, musical exposure in utero establishes a foundation for musical intelligence. Studies reveal that children exposed to music before birth demonstrate better musical abilities and auditory discrimination skills, suggesting that early auditory experiences can shape cognitive functions related to music and language.

2. Emotional and Social Development

The ability of the fetus to recognize the mother's voice plays a vital role in postnatal bonding. This early recognition fosters a sense of security and attachment, which are essential for healthy emotional and social development. The familiarity of the mother's voice can soothe the newborn, aiding in emotional regulation and stress reduction. This bonding process is crucial, as a secure attachment with caregivers forms the basis for future social relationships and emotional well-being. Early interactions and recognitions help infants develop trust and a sense of safety, which are foundational for exploring the world and forming social connections.

3. Motor Skills and Coordination

Prenatal tactile experiences are instrumental in the development of motor skills and coordination. Movements and tactile interactions within the womb help the fetus develop proprioception, which is the sense of body position and movement. This early development is essential for postnatal motor skills such as grasping, crawling, and walking. Fetuses exhibit habituation responses to repeated tactile stimuli, indicating early forms of learning and memory that contribute to motor skill development. These prenatal tactile experiences lay the groundwork for the physical coordination and motor abilities that are critical for interacting with the environment after birth.

- **Implications for Parenting and Educational Practices**

Understanding the significance of prenatal learning has important implications for parenting and educational practices. It emphasizes the need for a nurturing and stimulating prenatal environment to support optimal fetal development.

1. Maternal Health and Well-being

The mother's health and well-being are paramount in providing a conducive environment for prenatal learning. Adequate nutrition, stress management, and avoiding harmful substances like alcohol and tobacco are critical. Maternal stress can negatively impact fetal development, so creating a calm and positive environment is essential. Practices such as regular prenatal check-ups, healthy eating, exercise, and stress-relief techniques can enhance maternal well-being and, in turn, support fetal development.

2. Auditory Stimulation

Parents can enhance prenatal auditory learning by engaging in activities that promote auditory development. Talking to the fetus, playing music, and reading aloud can strengthen the auditory cortex and improve auditory discrimination skills. These activities also strengthen the parent-child bond, even before birth. Selecting calming and rhythmic music can soothe the fetus and have positive effects on emotional development. This early auditory stimulation can provide the fetus with a rich auditory environment that fosters cognitive and emotional growth.

3. Sensory Enrichment

Providing a varied diet introduces the fetus to different tastes and smells, promoting olfactory and gustatory learning. This exposure can influence the newborn's dietary preferences and acceptance of diverse foods, which is crucial for nutritional health. Maternal consumption of a range of healthy foods can ensure that the amniotic fluid carries various flavours, helping the fetus become accustomed to different tastes. This early sensory enrichment can pave the way for a more varied and balanced diet postnatally, supporting overall health and development.

- **Research and Future Directions**

The field of prenatal learning is still growing, and scientists continue to discover new ways that early experiences before birth shape a child's development. Future research is expected to look more closely at how genetic factors (the traits we inherit from our parents) and epigenetic factors (changes in gene expression influenced by the environment) affect prenatal learning. Additionally, researchers are interested in understanding how these early experiences impact the brain over a long time and developing strategies to help pregnancies at risk.

- **Genetic and Epigenetic Influences**

Scientists are studying how genetic and epigenetic factors interact with experiences in the womb to understand why children develop differently. Epigenetic changes, which are influenced by the prenatal environment, can have long-lasting effects on how genes are expressed and how a child develops. By learning more about these processes, researchers hope to create specific interventions that can support the best possible development for each child.

- **Long-term Outcomes**

To truly understand the impact of prenatal learning, researchers conduct long-term studies that follow people from before they are born until they become adults. These studies can show how early experiences in the womb affect cognitive abilities (like thinking and problem-solving), emotional health, and social behaviors throughout life. This information can help us understand the importance of prenatal learning for lifelong development.

- **Interventions and Support**

A crucial area of research is developing programs and interventions to support prenatal learning, especially for pregnancies that are at risk. For example, interventions might focus on reducing maternal stress, improving diet, and providing sensory stimulation during pregnancy. These programs aim to create a healthier environment for fetal development and reduce potential risks, ensuring that every child has the best start in life.

Conclusion

Prenatal learning plays a critical role in early childhood development, influencing cognitive, emotional, and social growth. Understanding the mechanisms and impacts of prenatal learning emphasizes the importance of a nurturing and stimulating prenatal environment. Parents, educators, and healthcare providers must recognize the significance of prenatal experiences and work together to support optimal development from the very beginning of life. As research continues to advance, new strategies and interventions will emerge, offering further opportunities to enhance prenatal learning and early childhood outcomes.

*****

3. The Impact of Maternal Stress on Fetal Development

Maternal stress, a significant issue in prenatal health, plays a critical role in shaping fetal development and subsequent child outcomes. Research in the past few decades has increasingly focused on understanding the intricate ways in which maternal stress can affect the developing fetus. This article delves into the various dimensions of maternal stress, the biological mechanisms involved, and the long-term implications for children's health and development.

"Addressing maternal stress through support networks, nutritional interventions, and mindfulness practices can significantly improve outcomes for both mother and child, paving the way for healthier generations."

Understanding Maternal Stress

Maternal stress refers to the psychological and physiological responses of pregnant women to challenging or threatening situations. This stress can arise from various sources, including financial hardships, relationship issues, work-related pressures, or health concerns. While a certain level of stress is a normal part of life, chronic or severe stress during pregnancy can have profound effects on both the mother and the developing fetus.

The way a mother's stress affects her unborn baby involves several biological processes. Here are the main pathways through which this happens:

Hypothalamic-Pituitary-Adrenal (HPA) Axis: The HPA axis is a system in the body that controls our response to stress. When a pregnant woman feels stressed, her body produces a hormone called cortisol. This hormone can cross the placenta, which is the organ that connects the mother and baby. High levels of cortisol in the mother's body can reach the baby and influence its development. If the baby is exposed to high cortisol levels for a long time, it can change how the baby's own stress response system develops. This might make the child more sensitive to stress after birth.

Placental Function: The placenta is crucial for the baby's development as it supplies nutrients and oxygen from the mother to the baby. Stress in the mother can change how the placenta works, affecting this vital transfer of nutrients and oxygen. Stress can also cause changes in the genes of the placenta, leading to the production of substances called inflammatory cytokines. These substances can affect the development of the baby's brain.

Immune System Modulation: Chronic stress can weaken the mother's immune system, making her more prone to infections. If a mother gets an infection during pregnancy, it can cause inflammation in her body. This inflammatory response has been linked to problems such as premature birth and developmental disorders in the child.

Epigenetic Modifications: Stress can cause changes in the way genes work without altering the DNA sequence itself. These changes, known as epigenetic modifications, include processes like DNA methylation and histone modification.

These modifications can have long-term effects on the child's health and development, potentially influencing how genes are expressed throughout the child's life.

- **Effects on Fetal Development**

The impact of maternal stress on fetal development manifests in various ways, influencing both physical and neurodevelopmental outcomes.

Physical Development:

Birth Weight: Maternal stress is associated with lower birth weight, a key indicator of neonatal health. Low birth weight increases the risk of infant mortality and can lead to long-term health issues such as cardiovascular disease and diabetes.

Preterm Birth: High levels of maternal stress are linked to an increased risk of preterm birth. Preterm infants face numerous challenges, including respiratory issues, feeding difficulties, and developmental delays.

Neurodevelopment:

Brain Development: Chronic maternal stress can affect fetal brain development, particularly in areas such as the hippocampus, prefrontal cortex, and amygdala. These regions are crucial for memory, executive function, and emotional regulation.

Behavioural Outcomes: Children exposed to high levels of prenatal stress are more likely to exhibit behavioural problems such as anxiety, depression, attention deficits, and hyperactivity. These issues can persist into adolescence and adulthood, impacting academic achievement and social relationships.

Long-term Implications for Child Development:

The effects of maternal stress during pregnancy can extend well beyond infancy, influencing various aspects of child development and health.

Cognitive Development:

Learning and Memory: Prenatal exposure to maternal stress can impair cognitive functions such as learning and memory. Children may show lower IQ scores and academic performance, which can affect their educational attainment and career prospects.

Attention and Executive Function: Stress-induced changes in brain development can lead to difficulties with attention, planning, and impulse control. These executive function deficits can contribute to challenges in school and daily life.

Emotional and Behavioural Health:

Emotional Regulation: Children exposed to high levels of prenatal stress may struggle with emotional regulation, leading to increased vulnerability to mood disorders such as anxiety and depression.

Social Interactions: Behavioural problems and emotional difficulties can hinder the development of healthy social relationships. Children may experience difficulties with peer interactions, leading to social isolation and low self-esteem.

Physical Health:

Metabolic Disorders: Prenatal stress is linked to an increased risk of metabolic disorders, including obesity and type 2 diabetes. These conditions can result from alterations in fetal programming and stress-induced changes in metabolic regulation.

Cardiovascular Health: Exposure to maternal stress can predispose children to cardiovascular issues later in life. Factors such as hypertension and altered lipid metabolism may contribute to the development of heart disease.

- **Mitigating the Effects of Maternal Stress**

While the impact of maternal stress on fetal development is profound, there are strategies that can help mitigate these effects and promote healthier outcomes for both mother and child.

Stress Management Interventions: One of the key strategies in mitigating maternal stress involves effective stress management interventions. Regular prenatal care and support from healthcare providers play a crucial role in identifying and addressing stressors early. These interventions can include counselling sessions, structured stress management programs, and the establishment of robust social support networks. Through these measures, pregnant women can receive the necessary guidance and emotional support to navigate the challenges of pregnancy more effectively.

In addition to professional support, mindfulness and relaxation techniques have shown considerable promise in reducing maternal stress. Practices such as mindfulness meditation, yoga, and deep breathing exercises can significantly lower stress levels and promote relaxation. By incorporating these techniques into their daily routines, pregnant women can enhance their overall well-being, thereby creating a more favourable intrauterine environment for fetal development.

Nutritional Support: Proper nutrition is another vital component in mitigating the effects of maternal stress on fetal development. A balanced diet rich in essential nutrients is fundamental to supporting both maternal and fetal health. Omega-3 fatty acids, found in fish and flaxseed, are particularly important for brain development. Ensuring a diet that includes a variety of fruits, vegetables, whole grains, and lean proteins can help maintain optimal health during pregnancy.

Supplementation with prenatal vitamins is also crucial in addressing any nutritional deficiencies that may arise. Key supplements such as folic acid, iron, and calcium support fetal growth and development. These vitamins and minerals play essential roles in preventing birth defects, promoting healthy bone development, and ensuring adequate oxygen transport to the fetus.

Physical Activity: Engaging in regular physical activity during pregnancy can have a profound impact on reducing maternal stress and improving overall health. Moderate exercise, such as walking, swimming, or prenatal yoga, helps release endorphins, which are natural stress relievers. Exercise also promotes better sleep, reduces anxiety, and enhances overall mood, contributing to a healthier pregnancy experience.

Physical activity during pregnancy not only benefits the mother but also supports fetal development. Regular exercise can improve circulation, ensuring that the fetus receives adequate oxygen and nutrients. It also helps maintain a healthy weight, reducing the risk of complications such as gestational diabetes and preeclampsia.

Social and Emotional Support: Strong social and emotional support systems are critical in buffering the effects of maternal stress. Support from family, friends, and community resources provides pregnant women with a sense of security and belonging, which can significantly reduce stress levels. Participation in support groups and parenting classes offers valuable information and emotional encouragement, helping women feel more prepared and confident as they approach motherhood.

Partner involvement is another essential aspect of social support. When partners actively participate in prenatal care and stress management, it enhances maternal well-being and fosters a supportive family environment. Partner support can alleviate feelings of isolation and provide practical assistance, further reducing the stress experienced during pregnancy.

Conclusion

The impact of maternal stress on fetal development is a complex and multifaceted issue that underscores the importance of maternal well-being during pregnancy. Understanding the biological mechanisms involved and the potential long-term effects on child development is crucial for developing effective interventions and support systems. By addressing maternal stress through comprehensive prenatal care, stress management strategies, and social support, we can promote healthier outcomes for both mothers and their children, ensuring a brighter future for the next generation.

*****

4. How to Implant a Growth Mindset Instead of a Fixed Mindset in Childhood

A mindset encompasses an individual's beliefs about their abilities and potential. According to psychologist Carol Dweck, who introduced the concepts of fixed and growth mindsets, these beliefs significantly influence how children approach challenges and learning. A fixed mindset implies a belief that abilities are static and unchangeable, leading to avoidance of challenges and fear of failure. In contrast, a growth mindset embraces the belief that abilities can be developed through dedication and hard work, fostering resilience and a love of learning. Implanting a growth mindset in childhood can have profound implications for a child's future success and happiness. This blog explores strategies for fostering a growth mindset in children.

"I have not failed. I've just found 10,000 ways that won't work." **- Thomas Edison**

Understanding Fixed vs. Growth Mindset

Fixed Mindset Characteristics:

Belief in Innate Talent: Children with a fixed mindset believe that intelligence and talent are inherent traits that cannot be developed.

Fear of Failure: They tend to avoid challenges to prevent failure and criticism.

Avoidance of Effort: They view effort as a sign of inadequacy, thinking that if something requires hard work, it means they aren't good at it.

Ignoring Constructive Feedback: They perceive constructive feedback as a personal attack rather than a tool for improvement.

- **Growth Mindset Characteristics**:

Belief in Development: Children with a growth mindset believe that intelligence and abilities can be developed through effort and learning.

Embracing Challenges: They see challenges as opportunities to grow and learn.

Valuing Effort: They understand that effort is essential for improvement and mastery.

Learning from Feedback: They use feedback as a guide to improve their skills and strategies.

- **Strategies for Implanting a Growth Mindset in Childhood**

Modelling a Growth Mindset: Children often mimic the attitudes and behaviours of adults, making it essential for parents and educators to model a growth mindset. This can be done by embracing challenges, learning from failures, and showing that effort leads to improvement. Positive self-talk is also crucial; instead of saying, "I can't do this," adults should use and encourage language that emphasizes growth and potential, such as, "I can't do this yet."

Praising the Process, Not the Person: When offering praise, focus on effort and strategies rather than innate abilities. Instead of saying, "You're so smart," say, "You worked really hard on that." This helps children understand that success comes from hard work and persistence. Commending persistence and resilience is equally important, as it highlights how these traits lead to improvement and success.

Encouraging a Love of Learning: Foster an environment where curiosity is encouraged, allowing children to explore new subjects and interests without the pressure of immediate success. Emphasize the importance of learning and personal growth over grades and scores, celebrating the acquisition of new knowledge and skills to instil a genuine love for learning.

Teaching the Value of Mistakes: Teach children that mistakes are a natural part of the learning process and should be viewed as opportunities to learn and grow. Encourage them to analyse their mistakes to understand what went wrong and how they can improve. This approach builds critical thinking and problem-solving skills.

Setting Realistic Goals and Celebrating Progress: Help children set small, achievable goals that lead to larger objectives. Celebrate progress towards these goals to build confidence and motivation. Encourage children to reflect on their growth and the progress they've made over time, reinforcing the idea that abilities can develop with effort.

Creating a Supportive Environment: Create an environment where children feel safe to take risks and make mistakes without fear of judgment. Promote cooperative learning, where children can work together, share strategies, and learn from one another, fostering a sense of community and mutual support.

Using Growth Mindset Language: Incorporate the "not yet" philosophy to indicate that while a child may not have mastered something now, they have the potential to do so with time and effort. Use phrases that emphasize growth potential, such as, "You haven't learned this yet, but you will with practice," to reinforce this mindset.

Providing Diverse Learning Opportunities: Offer a range of activities that cater to different interests and skill levels, allowing children to experience success in various domains. Present tasks that are challenging but achievable, helping children stretch their abilities and build confidence.

Incorporating Growth Mindset into Curriculum: Integrate lessons on brain plasticity, showing children that their brains can grow and change through learning and effort. Use stories of famous individuals who succeeded through persistence and hard work, reinforcing the value of a growth mindset. These curriculum elements help children internalize the belief that their abilities can be developed through dedication and effort.

- **Practical Activities to Foster a Growth Mindset**

Implementing practical activities to foster a growth mindset in children can be both engaging and effective. One such activity is maintaining **growth mindset journals**, where children document the challenges they face, how they address them, and the lessons they learn from these experiences. This reflective practice helps children recognize their growth and progress over time. Another beneficial activity is conducting goal-setting workshops, where children learn to set realistic goals and create actionable plans. This teaches them to break down larger tasks into manageable steps and celebrate their achievements, fostering a sense of accomplishment and motivation.

Mindset role-playing is another effective activity. By engaging in role-playing scenarios, children can practice responding to challenges and failures with a growth mindset, thinking of different strategies to overcome obstacles. Similarly, reading and discussing **mindset stories** can be impactful. These stories highlight characters who demonstrate a growth mindset, allowing children to relate to the characters' challenges, efforts, and eventual successes.

Brainstorming sessions can further encourage a growth mindset by allowing children to come up with creative solutions to problems. Praising their innovative ideas reinforces the value of creative thinking and effort. Implementing feedback circles, where children give and receive constructive feedback in a supportive environment, helps them view feedback as a positive tool for growth rather than criticism.

Finally, **displaying mindset posters** and visuals around classrooms and homes can serve as constant reminders of growth mindset principles. These can include quotes, images, and affirmations that inspire and remind children of the power of a growth mindset, reinforcing these concepts in their daily lives. By incorporating these practical activities, parents and educators can effectively nurture a growth mindset in children, setting the foundation for lifelong learning and resilience.

- **Addressing Challenges in Implanting a Growth Mindset**

Addressing the challenges in implanting a growth mindset requires a multi-faceted approach. Firstly, it is crucial to identify and manage situations that trigger a fixed mindset in children, such as high-stakes testing or overly critical feedback. Strategies must be developed to mitigate these triggers and consistently reinforce growth mindset principles. Secondly, fostering a growth mindset takes time, patience, and persistence. It is essential to consistently reinforce growth mindset concepts through daily interactions and practices, understanding that this transformation does not happen overnight. Thirdly, parental involvement is vital. Parents should be educated on the importance of a growth mindset and provided with resources and workshops to support their children's development at home. Engaging parents in this process ensures that the reinforcement of a growth mindset extends beyond the classroom. Lastly, professional development for educators is key. Providing opportunities for teachers to learn about growth mindset theory and practical implementation strategies ensures a cohesive and comprehensive approach across all areas of a child's life. This collective effort helps create an environment where children can thrive, embracing challenges and viewing failures as opportunities for growth.

Conclusion

Fostering a growth mindset in childhood lays the foundation for lifelong learning, resilience, and success. By modelling a growth mindset, praising the process, encouraging a love of learning, teaching the value of mistakes, setting realistic goals, creating a supportive environment, using growth mindset language, providing diverse learning opportunities, incorporating growth mindset into the curriculum, and engaging in practical activities, parents and educators can help children develop the belief that their abilities can grow with effort and perseverance. Overcoming challenges and involving all stakeholders in the process ensures that children are equipped with the mindset to thrive in an ever-changing world.

*****

5. Prenatal Bonding: Establishing Connection with Your Unborn Child

Prenatal bonding, the process of establishing a connection with your unborn child, is a vital part of the pregnancy journey. It encompasses the emotional and psychological interactions between a mother (and often the father or other family members) and the developing baby in the womb. This connection can have profound effects on both the parent and the child, influencing their relationship, the pregnancy experience, and even the child's development and well-being. This blog explores the importance, methods, and benefits of prenatal bonding, offering insights and practical tips for expectant parents.

"In the womb, your baby listens to your heartbeat, feels your emotions, and begins to know you. Prenatal bonding is the foundation of a lifetime of love and connection."

- **The Importance of Prenatal Bonding**

Prenatal bonding is crucial for several reasons. First, it helps expectant parents, particularly mothers, transition into their roles. Pregnancy is a period of significant physical and emotional change, and developing a bond with the unborn child can help mothers feel more connected to and prepared for motherhood.

For the unborn child, prenatal bonding can also be beneficial. Studies suggest that the emotional and psychological environment in the womb can impact the baby's development. A strong, positive bond can contribute to a healthier pregnancy, potentially leading to better outcomes for both mother and baby.

- **Psychological and Emotional Benefits**

Reduced Maternal Stress: Bonding activities, such as talking to the baby or engaging in relaxation exercises, can reduce maternal stress. Lower stress levels are beneficial for both the mother and the baby, as high stress can negatively impact fetal development.

Enhanced Emotional Well-being: Expectant mothers who feel connected to their unborn child often experience enhanced emotional well-being. This connection can alleviate feelings of anxiety and depression, fostering a more positive pregnancy experience.

Preparation for Parenthood: Prenatal bonding helps parents, especially first-time parents, prepare for the arrival of the baby. It allows them to start building a relationship with their child, which can ease the transition into parenthood and promote confidence in their parenting abilities.

- **Methods of Prenatal Bonding**

There are several ways expectant parents can bond with their unborn child. These methods are diverse and can be tailored to fit individual preferences and lifestyles.

1. Talking and Singing to the Baby

Talking and singing to the baby is one of the simplest and most effective ways to bond. The sound of the mother's voice is particularly soothing to the unborn child. Research indicates that babies can recognize and respond to their mother's voice from the womb.

Practical Tips:

Set aside a few minutes each day to talk to your baby. You can share your thoughts, read stories, or simply describe your day.

Singing lullabies or playing soft music can also be beneficial. Choose songs that you enjoy and that you find soothing.

2. Gentle Touch and Massage

Touch is another powerful tool for prenatal bonding. Gentle massage and caressing the belly can help mothers feel more connected to their babies.

Practical Tips:

Use circular motions to gently massage your belly, focusing on areas where you feel the baby's movements.

Encourage your partner to join in. This can help them feel more involved and connected to the baby.

3. Mindfulness and Meditation

Mindfulness and meditation practices can enhance the bond between mother and child by promoting relaxation and emotional connection.

Practical Tips:

Engage in daily mindfulness exercises. Focus on your breathing and visualize the baby inside you.

Use guided meditations specifically designed for pregnancy. These can help you connect with your baby on a deeper level.

4. Prenatal Yoga

Prenatal yoga combines physical exercise with relaxation techniques, making it an excellent practice for bonding with your unborn child. It helps mothers become more in tune with their bodies and their babies.

Practical Tips:

Join a prenatal yoga class or follow online sessions tailored for pregnancy.

Focus on breathing exercises and gentle stretches that promote relaxation and well-being.

5. Keeping a Pregnancy Journal

Writing a pregnancy journal allows mothers to document their thoughts, feelings, and experiences throughout pregnancy. This practice can foster a deeper connection with the unborn child.

Practical Tips:

Write regularly about your experiences, thoughts, and dreams for your baby.

Share your journal with your partner to involve them in the bonding process.

6. Visualization Techniques

Visualization techniques involve imagining your baby and your life together after birth. This practice can strengthen the emotional bond between mother and child.

Practical Tips:

Spend a few minutes each day visualizing your baby. Picture their face, their movements, and your interactions with them.

Use visualization during meditation or relaxation exercises.

- **Benefits of Prenatal Bonding for the Baby**

Prenatal bonding doesn't just benefit the parents; it also has positive effects on the unborn child. Here are some of the key benefits:

Enhanced Brain Development: The emotional connection and positive environment created through prenatal bonding can stimulate the baby's brain development. Babies who are frequently talked to and sung to in the womb show advanced auditory and language skills after birth.

Better Emotional Regulation: Babies who experience a strong bond with their mothers in utero are often better at regulating their emotions after birth. This can lead to a calmer, more content baby and can positively impact their temperament.

Stronger Parent-Child Relationship: Prenatal bonding lays the foundation for a strong parent-child relationship. Babies who feel loved and connected from the womb are more likely to form secure attachments with their parents after birth.

- **The Role of Fathers and Partners**

While much of the focus of prenatal bonding is on the mother, fathers and partners also play a crucial role. Their involvement can enhance the bonding experience and provide additional support to the mother.

Practical Tips for Fathers and Partners

Talk to the Baby: Fathers and partners should also spend time talking to the baby. This helps the baby recognize their voice and fosters a sense of connection.

Participate in Bonding Activities: Join the mother in activities like belly massage, attending prenatal classes, or practicing yoga. This shared experience can strengthen the bond with both the mother and the baby.

Support the Mother: Provide emotional and practical support to the mother. A stress-free and supported mother is more likely to engage in bonding activities.

Attend Ultrasound Appointments: Being present at ultrasound appointments can make the pregnancy feel more real and help partners feel more connected to the baby.

- **Cultural Perspectives on Prenatal Bonding**

Prenatal bonding practices vary widely across different cultures. Understanding these diverse practices can provide valuable insights and additional methods for bonding with your unborn child.

Indian Cultural Practices

In India, several traditional practices emphasize the importance of prenatal bonding:

Garbh Sanskar: This ancient practice involves a combination of music, meditation, and reading spiritual or positive literature to influence the baby's development positively. Garbh Sanskar promotes a calm and nurturing environment for both mother and child.

Rituals and Ceremonies: Traditional ceremonies like "Seemantham" in South India or "Godh Bharai" in North India are conducted to bless the mother and the unborn child. These rituals foster a sense of community and support around the pregnant woman.

Ayurvedic Practices: Ayurveda recommends specific dietary and lifestyle practices during pregnancy to ensure the well-being of the mother and baby. These include consuming nutritious foods, practicing gentle yoga, and engaging in relaxation techniques.

Western Cultural Practices

In Western cultures, prenatal bonding is often emphasized through scientific and psychological approaches:

Prenatal Classes: Many expectant parents attend prenatal classes that focus on childbirth education, baby care, and bonding techniques. These classes provide practical knowledge and support.

Technology and Gadgets: Devices like fetal dopplers and ultrasound scans are popular in Western cultures. These technologies allow parents to hear the baby's heartbeat and see their movements, enhancing the bonding experience.

Emphasis on Mental Health: Western cultures place a strong emphasis on the mental health of expectant mothers. Practices like mindfulness, therapy, and support groups are encouraged to promote emotional well-being and prenatal bonding.

- **Overcoming Challenges in Prenatal Bonding**

While prenatal bonding is a natural and beneficial process, some expectant parents may face challenges. These can include high levels of stress, medical complications, or emotional difficulties. It's important to address these challenges to ensure a healthy bonding experience.

Common Challenges

Stress and Anxiety: High levels of stress and anxiety can hinder the bonding process. It's crucial to manage stress through relaxation techniques, therapy, or support from loved ones.

Medical Complications: Complications like high-risk pregnancies can make bonding more challenging. In such cases, seeking medical advice and emotional support is essential.

Emotional Barriers: Some parents may struggle with emotional barriers, such as fear of miscarriage or unresolved trauma. Professional counselling can help address these issues and promote a healthy bonding experience.

Conclusion

Prenatal bonding is a crucial aspect of the pregnancy journey, offering numerous benefits for both the expectant parents and the unborn child. By engaging in bonding activities like talking, singing, gentle touch, mindfulness, and visualization, parents can establish a strong and nurturing connection with their baby. Fathers and partners also play a vital role in this process, providing support and enhancing the bonding experience.

Understanding the cultural perspectives and overcoming challenges can further enrich the prenatal bonding experience. With the right support and resources, expectant parents can create a positive and nurturing environment for their unborn child, laying the foundation for a strong and loving parent-child relationship. As you embark on this incredible journey, remember that every small effort you make to connect with your baby will have a lasting impact on both your lives.

*****

6. From Conception to Birth: The Incredible Story of Baby Brain Development

Once upon a time, in a cozy, warm place called the womb, a tiny little baby was under construction. This magical journey started the moment a tiny cell from the mother met a tiny cell from the father. Together, they formed a new cell, a single cell full of potential and promise. This was the very beginning of a brand new person.

As the weeks went by, the single cell began to divide and multiply, forming a cluster of cells. This growing cluster soon began to form different parts of the body. The most exciting part of this construction was the development of the baby's brain. Let's follow the journey of the baby's brain development and uncover some fascinating neurological facts about this little life.

> ***"The brain is an organ of remarkable complexity, growing from a few cells to a network of trillions of connections. The journey of its development begins even before birth, laying the foundation for every thought, feeling, and action."***

In the first few weeks, the baby is no bigger than a poppy seed. Yet, even at this tiny size, incredible things are happening. Around the third week after conception, a flat structure called the neural plate forms. This is the foundation of the baby's nervous system. Just a few days later, the neural plate folds in on itself to form the neural tube. The neural tube will eventually become the baby's brain and spinal cord.

Imagine a tiny construction site with workers laying down the initial beams and structures. That's what is happening inside the womb. These early stages are crucial because the neural tube needs to close properly. If it doesn't, it can lead to conditions like spina bifida, where the spinal cord doesn't develop correctly.

- **The First Trimester: The Brain Takes Shape**

As the baby grows to the size of a blueberry by the sixth week, the brain begins to take shape. By now, the neural tube has developed into three distinct sections: the forebrain, midbrain, and hindbrain. Each of these sections will grow and develop into different parts of the brain with specific functions.

The Forebrain: This part will eventually handle complex thinking, emotions, and memory.

The Midbrain: This area will process sensory information like sight and sound.

The Hindbrain: This region will control basic functions like breathing and heart rate.

Around the seventh week, neurons, which are the brain's building blocks, begin to form. Neurons are special cells that transmit information throughout the brain and body. Imagine them as tiny messengers running around delivering important notes.

- **The Second Trimester: Growth and Refinement**

By the time the second trimester begins, the baby is about the size of a peach. The brain is growing rapidly. During this period, the brain starts to develop folds and grooves. These wrinkles are called gyri and sulci, and they are essential because they increase the brain's surface area, allowing more neurons to fit inside the skull.

Around the 20th week, the baby can start to hear sounds. The tiny ears have developed enough to pick up noises from the outside world, like the mother's voice or music. This is possible because the auditory cortex, the part of the brain that processes sound, is now functioning.

Another fascinating development during this time is the formation of synapses. Synapses are the connections between neurons. They allow neurons to communicate with each other. Think of synapses as bridges that let the tiny messengers cross from one neuron to another. By the end of the second trimester, millions of these synaptic connections are forming every minute.

- **The Third Trimester: Final Touches**

As the third trimester begins, the baby is now about the size of a cantaloupe. The brain continues to grow and develop at an astonishing rate. The cerebral cortex, which is responsible for higher brain functions like thinking and planning, becomes more prominent. This part of the brain will continue to develop well into childhood.

By this stage, the baby's brain waves can be detected. These are the electrical signals that neurons use to communicate. Remarkably, the baby can even experience REM (Rapid Eye Movement) sleep, a sleep phase associated with dreaming. Although we can't know for sure, it's fun to imagine what the baby might be dreaming about in the womb.

Sensing the World

During the final weeks, the baby's brain is busy fine-tuning its senses. The visual cortex, responsible for sight, continues to develop, although the baby won't fully see until after birth. The baby's sense of touch is also becoming more refined. At this point, the baby can respond to gentle touches and may even grasp its tiny hands together.

The baby's brain is also preparing for language. Even though the baby won't speak until months after birth, the brain is already getting ready to process sounds and language patterns. Studies have shown that babies can recognize their mother's voice at birth, a testament to the incredible work the brain has done in the womb.

- **The Role of Nutrition and the Environment**

Throughout this construction process, the baby's brain development is heavily influenced by nutrition and the environment. The mother's diet plays a crucial role. Nutrients like folic acid, iron, and omega-3 fatty acids are vital for brain development. They help in the formation of neurons and the creation of synapses.

The mother's health and emotional state also impact the baby's brain. Stress can affect the hormones in the womb, which can, in turn, affect brain development. That's why it's important for expecting mothers to take care of their mental and physical health.

The Big Day: Birth

Finally, the day arrives when the baby is ready to meet the world. At birth, the baby's brain is about one-quarter the size of an adult brain but is packed with neurons - around 100 billion of them! Although the brain has made remarkable progress, it is still a work in progress. The brain will continue to grow and develop rapidly after birth, especially in the first few years of life. During this time, the baby's brain will form connections at an astonishing rate, laying the foundation for future learning and development. The baby's early experiences will be crucial in shaping their cognitive abilities, emotional responses, and overall brain function, highlighting the importance of a nurturing and stimulating environment.

After Birth: Continuing the Journey

Once the baby is born, the construction of the brain continues at a rapid pace. The experiences the baby has in the outside world will shape and refine the brain's structure. Each time the baby hears a new sound, sees a new face, or feels a new texture, new synapses form and strengthen. This period is characterized by intense brain activity, with the infant learning from every interaction and experience. These sensory experiences are critical for cognitive development, as they help the baby understand and interpret their surroundings. The brain's remarkable plasticity during this stage allows for rapid learning and adaptation, setting the stage for future intellectual and emotional growth.

- **The Importance of Early Experiences**

Early experiences are crucial for brain development. Positive interactions, such as being held, spoken to, and played with, help the brain develop properly. These experiences create a strong foundation for future learning, behaviour, and health.

In the first year, the brain doubles in size, and by the time the baby reaches three years old, it will be about 80% of its adult size. The connections that form during these early years set the stage for how the child will think, feel, and interact with the world.

Conclusion:

The Miracle of Brain Development

The journey of brain development from conception to birth is nothing short of miraculous. From a single cell to a complex organ capable of thought, emotion, and sensation, the brain's construction is a marvel of nature. Each stage of development is a testament to the incredible intricacy and precision required to build a functioning human brain.

As the baby grows and learns, the brain will continue to adapt and change, a process known as neuroplasticity. This lifelong ability of the brain to reorganize itself by forming new neural connections ensures that learning and growth continue throughout life.

So, next time you look at a baby, remember the incredible journey their brain has undergone. From a tiny cluster of cells to a bustling network of neurons and synapses, the construction of the brain is one of the most amazing feats of nature. And it all starts in the cozy, warm haven of the womb, where a tiny baby begins the incredible journey of life.

*****

7. 10 Genius Parenting Hacks That Will Change Your Life

Parenting is a journey filled with joy, challenges, and countless learning experiences. Every parent seeks ways to make their life easier while ensuring their child's well-being and happiness. Balancing daily responsibilities, nurturing growth, and maintaining a harmonious household can often feel overwhelming. However, with the right strategies, these tasks can become manageable and even enjoyable. Here, we present ten genius parenting hacks designed to streamline routines, promote independence, encourage learning, and foster a nurturing environment for your child, ultimately transforming your parenting experience for the better.

"The secret of your future is hidden in your daily routine." - **Mike Murdock**

1. The Magic of Routine Charts

Hack: Use visual routine charts to help children understand their daily schedule.

Routine charts are a fantastic tool to instil a sense of responsibility and independence in children. By visually mapping out their daily tasks—such as brushing their teeth, getting dressed, and completing homework—children can easily grasp what's expected of them. You can use images or simple words depending on the child's age.

How to Implement:

Create a colourful chart with a checklist of daily tasks.
Include pictures for younger children who cannot read yet.
Use stickers or markers to check off completed tasks.

Benefits:

Reduces morning and bedtime chaos.
Encourages self-discipline and time management skills.
Gives children a sense of accomplishment.

2. DIY Snack Stations

Hack: Set up DIY snack stations for kids to help themselves to healthy snacks.

Healthy snacking is important for growing children, and DIY snack stations empower them to make good food choices independently. Prepare small containers with a variety of snacks such as fruits, vegetables, cheese, and whole-grain crackers. Place these containers at child-friendly heights in the refrigerator and pantry.

How to Implement:

Use clear bins or containers to store snacks.
Label each container with the type of snack inside.
Rotate snack options regularly to keep things interesting.

Benefits:

Promotes healthy eating habits.
Reduces the need for constant parental assistance.
Encourages decision-making and autonomy.

3. Bedtime Story Recordings

Hack: Record yourself reading bedtime stories for nights when you can't be there.

Parents can't always be present for bedtime stories due to work commitments or other responsibilities. Recording yourself reading your child's favourite books ensures they still have a comforting bedtime routine even in your absence.

How to Implement:

Choose a variety of books your child loves.
Use a smartphone or recording device to record yourself reading each book.
Play these recordings at bedtime when needed.

Benefits:

Maintains a consistent bedtime routine.
Provides comfort and reassurance to your child.
Helps build a love for reading.

4. Clothing Coordination Simplified

Hack: Use a hanging organizer to pre-plan outfits for the week.

Morning routines can be hectic, especially when deciding what your child should wear each day. A hanging organizer with labelled compartments for each day of the week simplifies this process. Pre-select outfits and place them in the corresponding compartments to save time and reduce morning stress.

How to Implement:

Purchase a hanging organizer with at least seven compartments.
Label each compartment with the days of the week.
Involve your child in selecting outfits for the week.

Benefits:

Streamlines morning routines.
Teaches organizational skills.
Reduces decision-making stress.

5. Portable Art Kit

Hack: Create a portable art kit for on-the-go creativity.

Kids often need something to keep them occupied during travel, restaurant visits, or waiting rooms. A portable art kit filled with crayons, colouring books, stickers, and small craft supplies can provide hours of entertainment.

How to Implement:

Use a small, sturdy container or bag.
Include a variety of art supplies suited to your child's age.
Keep the kit handy for trips and outings.

Benefits:

Encourages creativity and artistic expression.
Keeps children entertained and occupied.
Reduces screen time.

6. Learning Through Play

Hack: Incorporate educational activities into playtime.

Children learn best when they're having fun. Integrate educational games and activities into their playtime to enhance their learning experiences. This could include puzzles, building blocks, or interactive apps that teach math, reading, and problem-solving skills.

How to Implement:

Choose toys and games that are both fun and educational.
Set aside specific times for educational play.
Join in on the play to guide and support your child's learning.

Benefits:

Promotes cognitive development.
Makes learning enjoyable and engaging.
Strengthens the parent-child bond through shared activities.

7. Color-Coded Organization

Hack: Use colour coding to organize toys, clothes, and school supplies.

Colour coding is a simple yet effective way to keep your home organized. Assign different colours to different categories of items, such as toys, clothes, and school supplies. This system helps children easily identify where things belong, making clean-up quicker and teaching organizational skills.

How to Implement:

Select a set of colours and assign each to a category.
Use coloured bins, labels, and stickers for organization.
Teach your child the color-coding system.

Benefits:

Simplifies the organization process.
Makes clean-up more efficient.
Encourages responsibility and tidiness.

8. Car Seat Command Center

Hack: Create a car seat command center to keep essentials within reach.

Long car rides can be challenging for both parents and children. A car seat command center keeps snacks, toys, books, and other essentials within arm's reach, making trips smoother and more enjoyable.

How to Implement:

Attach a backseat organizer to the front seat.
Stock it with snacks, water bottles, toys, and books.
Rotate the items regularly to keep things fresh and exciting.

Benefits:

Keeps children entertained during car rides.
Reduces the need for frequent stops.
Ensures essential items are always accessible.

9. The Toy Rotation System

Hack: Implement a toy rotation system to keep playtime exciting.

Children can quickly lose interest in their toys if they have too many available at once. A toy rotation system involves dividing toys into several groups and rotating them every few weeks. This keeps playtime exciting and helps manage toy clutter.

How to Implement:

Sort toys into several groups.
Store groups in separate bins out of sight.
Rotate the bins every few weeks.

Benefits:

Keeps children engaged with their toys.
Reduces toy clutter.
Encourages children to appreciate their toys more.

10. Positive Reinforcement Jar

Hack: Use a positive reinforcement jar to encourage good behaviour.

Positive reinforcement is a powerful tool for shaping behaviour. A positive reinforcement jar filled with marbles, coins, or small toys rewards good behaviour and motivates children to continue making positive choices.

How to Implement:

Choose a clear jar and fill it with small rewards.
Explain to your child how they can earn rewards for good behaviour.
Celebrate when the jar is filled and give a special reward.

Benefits:

Encourages positive behaviour.
Provides a visual representation of progress.
Strengthens the parent-child relationship through positive interactions.

Conclusion

Parenting is a dynamic and rewarding experience, and these ten hacks can help you navigate the challenges with ease. From establishing routines and promoting independence to encouraging learning and maintaining organization, these strategies are designed to create a smoother, more enjoyable parenting journey. Implementing these hacks will not only make your life easier but also foster a nurturing environment where your child can thrive. By incorporating these practical tips into your daily routine, you can enhance your parenting experience, reduce stress, and ensure your child's development is both positive and fulfilling.

*****

8. The Power of Play: Why It's Essential for Child Development

In a world increasingly dominated by structured activities, digital devices, and academic pressures, the simple joy of play often gets overlooked. Yet, play is not merely a laughing pastime for children; it is a fundamental component of healthy development. Play facilitates physical, emotional, social, and cognitive growth, providing a foundation for lifelong learning and well-being. This blog delves into the multifaceted benefits of play, emphasizing its irreplaceable role in child development.

"Play is often talked about as if it were a relief from serious learning. But for children, play is serious learning. Play is really the work of childhood." - Fred Rogers

The Definition and Types of Play

Play is an activity that is freely chosen, naturally motivated, and personally directed. It comes in various forms, each contributing uniquely to a child's growth:

Physical Play involves activities that engage the body through movement, such as running, jumping, and climbing. This form of play is vital for enhancing physical fitness, improving coordination, and developing motor skills. Through physical play, children build strong muscles and bones, improve their cardiovascular health, and refine their gross motor skills, which involve the larger muscles of the body. Additionally, fine motor skills, which involve smaller muscle groups, are honed through activities like drawing or playing with small objects. Physical play also helps children learn about their physical limits and how to manage risks safely.

Constructive Play is centered around creating or building something, such as constructing with blocks, drawing, or assembling puzzles. This type of play is crucial for fostering problem-solving skills and creativity. When children engage in constructive play, they learn to plan, experiment, and overcome challenges, which enhances their ability to think critically and innovate. Furthermore, constructive play improves fine motor skills as children manipulate small objects and tools, contributing to their overall sharpness and precision.

Fantasy or Pretend Play involves children immersing themselves in imaginative scenarios and taking on various roles and stories. This form of play is essential for developing language skills, as it encourages children to use and expand their vocabulary, construct sentences, and communicate effectively with others. Pretend play also fosters empathy and social understanding by allowing children to experience different perspectives and emotions. For instance, when playing house, children might take on the roles of different family members, which helps them understand and empathize with others' viewpoints and feelings.

Games with Rules include activities with structured guidelines, such as board games or organized sports. These games teach children about cooperation, strategy, and the importance of following directions. Participating in games with rules helps children learn to take turns, share, and work together towards a common goal. It also enhances their ability to strategize, plan ahead, and solve problems within a set framework. Through these activities, children develop social skills and learn to navigate the complexities of group dynamics and competition.

Cognitive Development Through Play

Play is a natural way for children to engage with the world around them, offering rich opportunities for cognitive development.

Enhancing Problem-Solving and Creativity: Through play, children encounter various challenges that require creative solutions. For instance, constructing a tower with blocks that won't fall or figuring out how to navigate a complex game scenario fosters critical thinking and innovation. These activities encourage children to experiment, make mistakes, and learn from them, thereby enhancing their problem-solving abilities and creativity.

Language and Communication Skills: Pretend play, in particular, is vital for developing language skills. When children engage in role-playing, they use language to negotiate roles, create stories, and express thoughts and emotions. This not only expands their vocabulary but also improves their ability to construct sentences and communicate effectively.

Conceptual Understanding and Academic Skills: Play also contributes to the development of academic skills in an engaging and stress-free manner. For example, board games can introduce basic math concepts such as counting, addition, and subtraction. Similarly, puzzles and building blocks can enhance spatial awareness and geometry skills. Through play, children develop a conceptual understanding of various subjects, laying a solid foundation for future academic success.

Physical Development and Health Benefits

Physical play is crucial for the healthy growth of a child's body. It promotes physical fitness, improves motor skills, and contributes to overall health and well-being.

Motor Skills and Coordination: Activities such as running, jumping, and climbing help develop gross motor skills, which involve the larger muscles of the body. Fine motor skills, which involve the smaller muscles, are enhanced through activities like drawing, cutting with scissors, and manipulating small objects. Both types of motor skills are essential for performing everyday tasks and participating in sports and other physical activities.

Health and Fitness: Engaging in physical play helps children maintain a healthy weight and build strong bones and muscles. It also promotes cardiovascular health and helps prevent childhood obesity. Regular physical activity is associated with numerous health benefits, including improved sleep, reduced stress, and a lower risk of developing chronic diseases later in life.

Understanding Boundaries and Safety: Physical play also teaches children about their physical limits and the importance of safety. For instance, when climbing a tree or playing in a jungle gym, children learn to assess risks and make decisions that keep them safe. This understanding of personal boundaries and safety is crucial for their overall well-being.

Emotional and Social Development

Play is a powerful tool for emotional and social development, helping children understand their own emotions and those of others, develop social skills, and build strong relationships.

Emotional Regulation and Resilience: Through play, children experience a range of emotions, from joy and excitement to frustration and disappointment. Learning to cope with these emotions in a safe and supportive environment helps children develop emotional regulation skills. For instance, a child might feel frustrated when a tower of blocks falls, but through repeated attempts and eventual success, they learn persistence and resilience.

Empathy and Understanding: Pretend play allows children to step into different roles and perspectives, fostering empathy and social understanding. For example, when playing house, children take on roles such as parent or sibling, which helps them understand different viewpoints and develop empathy. This ability to empathize with others is crucial for forming healthy relationships and navigating social interactions.

Social Skills and Cooperation: Play often involves interaction with peers, which helps children develop essential social skills such as cooperation, negotiation, and conflict resolution. Games with rules, for instance, teach children about taking turns, following rules, and working together towards a common goal. These experiences are invaluable for developing positive social behaviours and forming lasting friendships.

- **The Role of Adults in Facilitating Play**

While play is intrinsically motivated and directed by children, adults play a crucial role in facilitating and supporting it.

Creating a Play-Friendly Environment: Adults can create environments that encourage and support play by providing safe spaces and a variety of materials. This might include setting up a playground, providing art supplies, or simply offering a variety of toys that stimulate imagination and creativity. A play-friendly environment allows children to explore, experiment, and engage in different types of play.

Encouragement and Participation: Encouragement and active participation from adults can enhance the quality of play. By showing interest and engaging in play activities with children, adults can model positive behaviours, introduce new concepts, and provide guidance when needed. However, it's important for adults to strike a balance between involvement and allowing children the freedom to direct their own play.

Recognizing the Value of Play: Adults, including parents, educators, and policymakers, need to recognize the intrinsic value of play and advocate for its inclusion in daily routines and educational settings. This means not only providing time and space for play but also understanding that play is not a break from learning—it is learning.

- **Challenges to Play in the Modern World**

Despite its importance, play faces several challenges in the modern world, from busy schedules and academic pressures to the rise of digital technology.

Time Constraints and Structured Activities: Many children today have busy schedules filled with structured activities such as organized sports, music lessons, and academic tutoring. While these activities have their own benefits, they can limit the time available for unstructured play. It's important for parents and educators to strike a balance, ensuring that children have ample time for free play.

Digital Distractions: The rise of digital technology has introduced new forms of play, such as video games and online activities. While these can offer cognitive benefits, they often lack the physical and social aspects of traditional play. Excessive screen time can also lead to sedentary lifestyles and reduce opportunities for face-to-face interactions. Encouraging a balanced approach to technology use, where digital play complements rather than replaces traditional play, is essential.

Academic Pressures: In many educational systems, there is a growing emphasis on academic achievement and standardized testing, often at the expense of play. However, numerous studies have shown that play-based learning can be just as effective, if not more so, in promoting academic skills and overall development. Schools and educators should advocate for a more balanced approach that integrates play into the curriculum.

Conclusion

The power of play in child development cannot be overstated. It is a vital component that supports cognitive, physical, emotional, and social growth. Through play, children learn to solve problems, communicate effectively, regulate their emotions, and interact socially. Despite the challenges posed by modern life, it is crucial for parents, educators, and policymakers to prioritize and advocate for play. By doing so, we ensure that children have the opportunity to grow into well-rounded, healthy, and resilient individuals. Play is not just an activity; it is a foundation for lifelong learning and well-being.

*****

9. Why Self-Care Isn't Selfish: A Must-Read for Exhausted Parents

Parenting is one of the most rewarding yet toughest jobs out there. Parents often put their children's needs first, but in doing so, they can forget to take care of themselves. This can lead to stress, exhaustion, and even resentment. Taking care of yourself, known as self-care, isn't selfish; it's crucial. When parents look after their own mental and physical health, they become better, happier, and more effective in raising their children. This blog will explain why self-care is important for parents and how it can make a big difference in their lives and their children's lives.

"Taking care of yourself doesn't mean me first; it means me too." **- L.R. Knost**

- **The Myth of Selfishness**

Understanding Self-Care: Self-care encompasses a range of activities and practices that individuals engage in to reduce stress and enhance their overall well-being. These activities can vary greatly in complexity and time commitment. For example, self-care can be as simple as taking a few minutes to savour a cup of tea in peace, allowing a brief break from the day's demands. On the other end of the spectrum, it can involve more structured practices such as scheduling regular therapy sessions to address mental health needs. Regardless of the form it takes, self-care is not an indulgence; it is a fundamental necessity for maintaining health and balance in life. This misconception that self-care is a luxury often prevents parents from prioritizing their own needs, mistakenly believing that their sole focus should be on their children's well-being.

The Guilt Trap: Many parents are caught by the guilt trap, a pervasive belief that any time devoted to self-care is time stolen from their children. This guilt is rooted in the misconception that good parenting requires constant availability and self-sacrifice. While the instinct to put children's needs first is natural and commendable, it is important to recognize that neglecting one's own needs can lead to significant negative consequences. Parents who do not take time for themselves risk experiencing burnout, which can manifest as physical exhaustion, emotional fatigue, and increased irritability. Over time, this state of depletion can foster resentment and a diminished capacity to engage effectively with their children. Instead of enhancing their parenting, the guilt-driven neglect of self-care ultimately undermines it.

- **The Importance of Self-Care**

Mental Health Benefits: Maintaining mental health is crucial for effective parenting. Engaging in self-care activities such as mindfulness, meditation, and hobbies can significantly reduce stress and anxiety levels. These practices provide parents with essential tools to manage their mental well-being, which in turn helps them remain patient, understanding, and better equipped to tackle the inevitable challenges of parenting. A mentally healthy parent is more resilient and capable of providing the stable and nurturing environment that children need.

Physical Health Benefits: Physical well-being is equally vital for parents. Regular exercise, sufficient sleep, and proper nutrition are key components of self-care that contribute to overall physical health. When parents neglect these aspects of their health, they become more vulnerable to illnesses and chronic fatigue. This physical decline can make it increasingly difficult to keep up with the demands of parenting. By prioritizing their physical health, parents ensure they have the energy and stamina necessary to care for their children effectively.

Modelling Healthy Behaviour: Children are keen observers and often imitate the behaviours they see in their parents. By prioritizing self-care, parents model healthy behaviours, demonstrating the importance of taking care of oneself. This positive example helps children understand and develop good self-care habits that will benefit them throughout their lives. When children see their parents engaging in self-care without guilt, they learn that it is an important and acceptable part of a balanced life. This modelling not only benefits the children in the short term but also instils lifelong habits that contribute to their future well-being.

- **Practical Self-Care Strategies for Parents**

Time Management: Practical self-care strategies for parents encompass various facets, beginning with effective time management. With the relentless demands of parenting, prioritizing tasks becomes paramount. Identifying the most crucial responsibilities and focusing on them allows parents to let go of perfectionism and accept that not everything can be accomplished in a day. Delegating tasks to partners, older children, or family members lighten the load, promoting a more balanced approach to daily responsibilities. Moreover, scheduling self-care activities as non-negotiable appointments ensures they receive the attention they deserve amidst the chaos of daily life. Whether it's dedicating time for a workout, indulging in a hobby, or simply enjoying quiet moments, blocking out time on the calendar reinforces the importance of self-care.

Mindfulness and Relaxation Techniques: Mindfulness and relaxation techniques are indispensable tools for parents striving to maintain their equilibrium. Incorporating meditation into daily routines, even for just a few minutes, can significantly reduce stress and enhance focus. Similarly, practicing deep breathing exercises offers a simple yet effective way to calm the mind and body, fostering a sense of inner peace. Additionally, engaging in yoga not only provides physical benefits but also promotes mindfulness, making it an excellent avenue for relaxation and fitness.

Social Support: Building a robust support network is another crucial aspect of self-care for parents. Connecting with other parents allows for the sharing of experiences and advice, providing valuable insights and emotional support. Seeking professional help from therapists or counsellors is essential for addressing stress, anxiety, or depression effectively. Furthermore, leaning on family and friends for support, whether through babysitting assistance or lending an empathetic ear, reinforces the notion that it's okay to ask for help and strengthens familial bonds.

Pursuing Hobbies and Interests: Pursuing hobbies and interests is vital for nurturing one's well-being. Engaging in creative activities such as painting, writing, or playing music offers a therapeutic outlet for expression and self-discovery. Similarly, participating in physical activities like sports, hiking, or dancing not only improves physical health but also uplifts mood and boosts energy levels. Additionally, allocating time for reading or learning something new provides intellectual stimulation and a welcome respite from the routine demands of parenthood.

- **Overcoming Barriers to Self-Care**

Addressing Guilt: Guilt, a common feeling among parents when prioritizing their own well-being, can be particularly challenging to overcome. To combat this, it's crucial for parents to reframe their thinking and understand that self-care isn't selfish but rather a necessary investment in their family's overall health and happiness. A parent who is well-rested, healthy, and content is far more capable of providing the care and support their family needs compared to one who is exhausted and overwhelmed.

Managing Expectations: Another barrier to self-care is managing societal expectations, especially those placed on mothers. Society often imposes unrealistic standards on parents, leading to feelings of inadequacy and guilt when they prioritize themselves. It's essential for parents to recognize these pressures and set realistic expectations for themselves. Learning to say no and establishing boundaries is not only acceptable but necessary for maintaining one's well-being.

Financial Constraints: Financial constraints can also hinder parents from engaging in self-care activities, as many assume that self-care requires significant financial investment. However, self-care doesn't have to be expensive. There are numerous cost-effective or even free self-care practices available, such as taking a walk in nature, practising meditation, or spending quality time with loved ones. Seeking out community-based resources, like local yoga classes, online therapy services, or support groups, can provide valuable support without breaking the bank. By embracing these alternatives, parents can prioritize self-care without adding financial strain to their lives.

- **The Long-Term Benefits of Self-Care**

Improved Parenting Skills: Improved parenting skills are a direct result of self-care practices. When parents take the time to care for themselves, they cultivate patience, empathy, and engagement. They develop emotional resilience, enabling them to navigate the challenges and uncertainties of parenting with grace and composure. Moreover, by modelling positive behaviour through their self-care routines, they instil valuable lessons in self-love and self-respect in their children, laying the foundation for healthy emotional development.

Strengthened Relationships: Self-care contributes to strengthened relationships within the family unit and beyond. As parents prioritize their own well-being, they become better partners and friends. Strong relationships are built on a foundation of mutual respect, understanding, and support, qualities that are nurtured through self-care practices. By prioritizing their own needs alongside those of their family, parents create an atmosphere of reciprocity and mutual care within their relationships. This, in turn, fosters a more harmonious family environment, characterized by open communication, emotional support, and shared experiences.

Enhanced Quality of Life: The long-term benefits of self-care culminate in an enhanced overall quality of life for parents and their families. When individuals prioritize their well-being, they experience greater happiness, health, and fulfilment. This positivity radiates throughout their interactions with their children, creating a more joyful and nurturing home environment. By prioritizing self-care, parents demonstrate to their children the importance of self-love and self-respect, empowering them to lead balanced and fulfilling lives themselves. In essence, self-care isn't just about individual well-being—it's about building stronger families, healthier relationships, and a more vibrant community for generations to come.

Conclusion

Self-care is not a selfish act; it's an essential component of effective parenting. By taking care of their physical, mental, and emotional well-being, parents can be the best versions of themselves for their children. Overcoming the guilt and societal pressures associated with self-care can be challenging, but the benefits are well worth the effort. Remember, a happy parent raises happy children. So, prioritize self-care and embrace the journey of parenthood with renewed energy and joy.

******

10. Raising Resilient Kids: How to Foster Grit and Determination

In a world characterized by rapid change and uncertainty, the ability to persevere and remain steadfast in the face of adversity has never been more critical. Resilience, grit, and determination are not just buzzwords; they are essential skills that empower children to navigate life's challenges successfully. Raising resilient kids who can face setbacks with strength and bounce back from difficulties is one of the most valuable gifts parents can offer. This blog explores practical strategies and insights on how to foster these traits in children, helping them grow into determined and resilient adults.

"Grit is passion and perseverance for very long-term goals. Grit is having stamina. Grit is sticking with your future, day in, day out, not just for the week, not just for the month, but for years, and working really hard to make that future a reality." - Angela Duckworth

Understanding Resilience, Grit, and Determination

Resilience is the ability to recover from setbacks and adapt to difficult circumstances. It involves emotional strength, mental fortitude, and the capacity to bounce back from failure. Grit, as defined by psychologist Angela Duckworth, is a combination of passion and perseverance for long-term goals. It's about maintaining effort and interest over the years despite failure, adversity, and plateaus in progress. Determination is the firmness of purpose and the resolve to achieve one's goals despite obstacles.

These traits are interlinked and collectively contribute to a child's ability to handle stress, overcome challenges, and achieve long-term success.

The Role of Parents and Caregivers

Parents and caregivers play a crucial role in developing resilience and grit in children. This responsibility involves creating a supportive environment, modelling resilient behaviour, and providing opportunities for children to experience and overcome challenges.

1. Modelling Resilience and Grit

Children learn significantly through imitation and observation. When parents exhibit resilience and grit, they provide a tangible example for their children. Here's how parents can model these traits effectively:

Demonstrate Perseverance: Let your children see you tackle challenges head-on. Share stories from your own life where you faced difficulties but persisted until you succeeded. For instance, if you faced a tough project at work, explain how you managed stress, sought solutions, and ultimately overcame the obstacle.

Open Communication: Discuss your failures and setbacks openly with your children. Explain what you learned from these experiences and how they contributed to your growth. This helps children understand that failure is a natural part of life and a stepping stone to success.

Maintain a Positive Attitude: Show how you stay optimistic even during tough times. Your attitude towards setbacks can teach children the importance of maintaining hope and determination, even when things are challenging.

2. Encouraging a Growth Mindset

The concept of a growth mindset, introduced by psychologist Carol Dweck, emphasizes the belief that abilities and intelligence can be developed through dedication and hard work. Here's how to foster a growth mindset in your children:

Praise Effort Over Talent: Focus on praising the effort your child puts into their activities rather than their innate abilities. For example, instead of saying, "You're so smart," you could say, "You worked really hard on that project, and it shows."

Teach the Value of Challenges: Encourage your child to embrace challenges as opportunities to learn and grow. Explain that struggling with difficult tasks is a part of the learning process and can lead to improvement over time.

Provide Constructive Feedback: Offer specific, constructive feedback that highlights areas for improvement while acknowledging effort. Instead of generic praise, say, "I noticed you kept trying different strategies to solve that math problem. Great persistence!"

3. Creating a Safe and Supportive Environment

A nurturing and secure environment is crucial for building resilience in children. Here are some ways to create such an environment:

Emotional Safety: Make sure your child feels safe expressing their emotions without fear of judgment or punishment. Listen actively and empathetically when they share their feelings and concerns.

Consistent Support: Be a reliable source of support. Show your child that you are there for them, whether they succeed or fail. This consistent support helps them feel secure enough to take risks.

Encouraging Independence: While support is essential, it's also important to encourage independence. Allow your child to try new things on their own, make decisions, and solve problems. This fosters a sense of competence and autonomy.

4. Promoting Healthy Risk-Taking

Encouraging children to take healthy risks helps them build confidence and learn that failure is a natural part of growth. Here's how to promote healthy risk-taking:

Encourage Exploration: Support your child in trying new activities, whether it's a new sport, musical instrument, or social activity. This exposure helps them discover their interests and strengths.

Set Achievable Goals: Help your child set realistic but challenging goals. Break these goals into smaller, manageable steps to prevent them from feeling overwhelmed. Celebrate their progress and milestones along the way.

Teach Coping Skills: Equip your child with strategies to handle failure and setbacks. This could include problem-solving techniques, stress management skills, and ways to stay motivated despite difficulties.

Normalize Failure: Share stories of well-known figures who faced repeated failures before achieving success. Explain how these individuals used their experiences as learning opportunities. This can help children view failure as a part of the journey to success rather than a final defeat.

By integrating these strategies into daily life, parents can effectively foster resilience, grit, and determination in their children, preparing them to face life's challenges with confidence and perseverance.

- **The Role of Education and Extracurricular Activities**

Schools and extracurricular activities play a significant role in developing resilience and grit. Educational environments that challenge students and provide opportunities for growth contribute to building these traits.

Academic Challenges: Schools serve as environments where students are continually exposed to academic challenges that are designed to stretch their abilities. When students encounter difficulties in their academic pursuits, they have the opportunity to develop resilience by persisting through these challenges. Educational institutions that foster a growth mindset, emphasizing the belief that intelligence and abilities can be developed through dedication and hard work, play a crucial role in instilling resilience. Moreover, schools that offer support mechanisms for struggling students, such as tutoring programs or counselling services, create an environment where students feel empowered to overcome obstacles and succeed. Through overcoming academic challenges, students not only enhance their academic skills but also cultivate resilience that can be applied to various aspects of their lives.

Sports and Team Activities: Participation in sports and team activities provides invaluable lessons in resilience and grit. These activities often involve facing adversity, whether it be in the form of defeat, injuries, or setbacks during training. Through sports, children learn the importance of perseverance, as they must continue to practice and improve despite facing obstacles. Additionally, team sports emphasize the significance of collaboration and teamwork, as success often hinges on the collective effort of the team rather than individual performance. Learning to work together towards a common goal fosters resilience by teaching children how to support one another and navigate challenges collectively. Moreover, experiencing defeat in sports teaches individuals how to handle failure gracefully, reinforcing the idea that setbacks are opportunities for growth rather than indicators of inadequacy.

Arts and Creative Pursuits: Engaging in arts and creative activities provides an outlet for self-expression and a means of coping with stress. Whether through visual arts, music, dance, or theatre, creative pursuits allow individuals to channel their emotions and thoughts into tangible forms of expression. In the process of creating art, individuals often encounter challenges that require persistence and dedication to overcome. Whether it's perfecting a musical piece, refining a painting, or mastering a dance routine, the journey of artistic creation instils a sense of resilience by teaching individuals to persevere through difficulties. Furthermore, the creative process fosters a growth mindset by emphasizing experimentation and learning from mistakes. By encouraging individuals to embrace failure as a natural part of the creative process, arts education cultivates resilience and grit that can be applied beyond the realm of artistic endeavours.

- **The Role of Community and Society**

Communities and societal institutions also play a crucial role in fostering resilience and grit in children. Creating environments that support and challenge children is a collective responsibility.

Community Programs: Community programs serve as platforms for children to engage in various activities that promote social skills, teamwork, and leadership. These programs create spaces where children can interact with peers from diverse backgrounds, learn to collaborate, communicate effectively, and develop empathy. Activities such as volunteering not only contribute to the betterment of society but also instil in children a sense of purpose and accomplishment. By participating in community programs, children learn the value of contributing to their communities and gain a deeper understanding of their role in society.

Mentorship Opportunities: Mentorship connects children with experienced individuals who can provide guidance, support, and inspiration. Mentors serve as role models, offering valuable life lessons and sharing their own experiences of overcoming challenges. Through mentorship, children learn resilience by observing how their mentors navigate adversity and setbacks. Mentors also provide a supportive relationship outside of the family environment, offering encouragement and helping children build confidence in their abilities. These relationships often extend beyond childhood, providing ongoing support and guidance as children grow into adulthood.

Conclusion

Raising resilient kids who embody grit and determination is a multifaceted endeavour that requires the involvement of parents, educators, and the community. By modelling resilience, encouraging a growth mindset, and providing opportunities for children to face and overcome challenges, we can equip them with the tools they need to succeed. In an ever-changing world, these traits will help them navigate obstacles and achieve their full potential. By fostering resilience and grit in our children, we invest in a future generation capable of facing adversity with strength, perseverance, and unwavering determination. The journey to resilience is ongoing, and with the right support, every child has the potential to become a resilient and determined individual, ready to conquer the challenges that lie ahead.

*****

11. The Unseen Sacrifice: Why Indian Mothers Prioritize Their Children Over Themselves

Indian mothers are often celebrated for their selflessness and dedication, traits that are deeply rooted in the cultural fabric of India. This phenomenon of mothers prioritizing their children over their own well-being is a complex issue influenced by historical, cultural, societal, and economic factors. This blog delves into the multifaceted reasons behind this self-sacrificial behaviour, exploring the role of tradition, societal expectations, and the intrinsic values embedded within Indian society.

"The moment a child is born, the mother is also born. She never existed before. The woman existed, but the mother, never. A mother is something absolutely new." - **Rajneesh**

Cultural and Historical Context

To understand why Indian mothers often neglect their own needs in favour of their children, it is crucial to examine the cultural and historical backdrop. Historically, Indian society has been predominantly male-controlled, where women's roles were largely confined to the domestic sphere. The ancient texts and scriptures, while respecting motherhood, also placed the mother in a position of selfless devotion to her family. This cultural narrative has been perpetuated over centuries, embedding the idea of the self-sacrificing mother deeply into the collective consciousness.

In Indian mythology and epics like the Ramayana and Mahabharata, mothers are often depicted as the epitome of selflessness and sacrifice. These stories, passed down through generations, reinforce the notion that a good mother puts her children's needs above her own. For instance, the character of Kunti in the Mahabharata symbolizes the ultimate maternal sacrifice, often foregoing her own desires for the sake of her sons.

- **Societal Expectations and Gender Roles**

The societal expectations placed on Indian women further intensify this trend. From a young age, girls are often socialized to be nurturing and self-sacrificing. They are taught that their primary role in life is to be good wives and mothers. This social conditioning is reinforced through various means, including family, education, and media.

In many Indian families, the well-being of the children is considered the mother's foremost responsibility. This expectation is so deeply ingrained that mothers often feel immense pressure to conform to this ideal, fearing social isolation or criticism if they prioritize their own needs. The judgment is not just external; it is internalized, leading many mothers to genuinely believe that neglecting their own health and well-being is a virtue.

Economic Factors

Economic constraints also play a significant role in why Indian mothers often prioritize their children over themselves. In many Indian households, especially in lower-income families, resources are limited. When faced with financial constraints, mothers often choose to allocate available resources to their children, sacrificing their own needs in the process.

For instance, in many rural and economically disadvantaged households, healthcare and nutrition are areas where mothers commonly make sacrifices. If there is only enough food for either the children or the mother to eat adequately, the mother will often ensure that her children eat well. Similarly, if a family can afford only one medical treatment, it is usually the children who receive it. This economic sacrifice is viewed as an integral part of maternal duty.

Psychological Factors

The psychological aspect of motherhood also cannot be ignored. Many Indian mothers derive their sense of identity and self-worth from their role as caregivers. Their happiness and fulfilment are often tied to their children's well-being and success. This emotional investment can lead to a situation where they neglect their own needs, as they feel that their primary source of joy and purpose is the welfare of their children.

Moreover, the concept of "good motherhood" in Indian culture is often equated with selflessness and sacrifice. Mothers who prioritize their children's needs above their own are praised and respected, while those who do not may face criticism and judgement. This societal validation reinforces the behaviour, making it a deeply ingrained part of their identity.

- **Impact of Education and Employment**

Education and employment opportunities for women have increased in India over the years, yet these changes have not significantly altered the expectations placed on mothers.

Even working mothers are often expected to balance their professional responsibilities with their traditional roles at home. The dual burden of work and domestic duties can lead to further neglect of personal health and well-being.

In many cases, working mothers in India face a dilemma. They strive to excel in their careers to provide better opportunities for their children, yet they also adhere to societal norms that expect them to be the primary caregivers. This double burden often results in burnout and neglect of personal health, as they prioritize their children and work over their own needs.

- **The Role of Extended Families**

In India, the concept of joint families is still prevalent, where multiple generations live under one roof. While this setup can provide support and assistance, it also comes with its own set of challenges. Mothers, especially daughters-in-law, are often expected to take care of the entire family, including elderly parents and in-laws, in addition to their own children. This extended caregiving role leaves little time for self-care.

In such family structures, the hierarchical system often places the mother-in-law at the top, with the younger mother assuming a more obedient role. This dynamic can further pressure mothers to prioritize the needs of the family over their own, as failing to do so might result in familial discord or disapproval.

Health Implications

The neglect of self-care among Indian mothers has significant health implications. Chronic stress, fatigue, and mental health issues like depression and anxiety are common among mothers who continually place their children's needs above their own. Physical health problems, such as malnutrition, untreated medical conditions, and lack of exercise, are also prevalent.

Despite these health risks, many mothers do not seek medical help for themselves, either due to financial constraints or the belief that their health is secondary to their children's. This neglect can lead to severe long-term health consequences, impacting their ability to care for their families in the future.

- **Changing Trends**

Increasing Awareness about Self-Care: As society becomes more educated and interconnected, there is a growing recognition of the importance of self-care and mental health. This awareness is gradually permeating societal attitudes, challenging the traditional notion of the self-sacrificing mother. Women are beginning to realize that neglecting their own well-being ultimately undermines their ability to care for their families effectively.

Empowerment of Younger Generations: Younger generations of women in India are more educated, ambitious, and career-oriented than their predecessors. They are challenging the traditional gender roles and expectations that have long confined women to the domestic sphere. With increased access to education and economic opportunities, these women are asserting their autonomy and questioning the narrative that equates motherhood solely with self-sacrifice.

Women's Empowerment Movements: Women's empowerment movements in India are gaining momentum, advocating for gender equality, women's rights, and empowerment. These movements provide a platform for women, including mothers, to assert their rights and demand recognition for their contributions beyond caregiving. By challenging male-controlled norms and promoting women's autonomy, these movements are instrumental in reshaping societal attitudes towards motherhood.

Impact of Social Media: The rise of social media platforms has transformed the way individuals communicate and share information. For mothers in India, social media has become a powerful tool for connecting with other women, sharing experiences, and seeking support. These platforms provide a virtual community where mothers can discuss their struggles openly, without fear of judgment or stigma. Social media also serves as a platform for advocacy, raising awareness about the importance of self-care and mental health among mothers.

- **The Way Forward**

Promoting Self-Care Education: Education plays a crucial role in promoting self-care among Indian mothers. Schools, community centers, and healthcare facilities can implement programs aimed at educating women about the importance of self-care practices, including proper nutrition, exercise, and mental health management. By equipping women with the knowledge and resources to prioritize their own well-being, we can empower them to make healthier choices for themselves and their families.

Supporting Work-Life Balance: Employers and policymakers can take steps to support working mothers in achieving a healthy work-life balance. Flexible work arrangements, affordable childcare options, and parental leave policies can help lessen the burden on mothers, allowing them to balance their professional and personal responsibilities more effectively. By creating a supportive environment for working mothers, we can enable them to prioritize their own health and well-being without sacrificing their careers or financial security.

Fostering a Culture of Empowerment: Creating a culture that values and empowers women is essential for promoting self-care among mothers. This involves challenging traditional gender norms and expectations, promoting women's autonomy and agency, and recognizing the diverse roles and contributions of women in society. By fostering a culture of empowerment and equality, we can create an environment where mothers feel empowered to prioritize their own needs alongside those of their children.

Investing in Mental Health Services: Access to mental health services is essential for supporting the well-being of mothers in India. Governments, NGOs, and healthcare organizations can invest in expanding mental health infrastructure and services, making them more accessible and affordable for women, especially those from marginalized communities. By providing women with the support and resources they need to address their mental health concerns, we can promote overall well-being for mothers and their families.

Conclusion

The self-sacrificial nature of Indian mothers is a deeply ingrained cultural phenomenon influenced by historical, societal, and economic factors. While this behaviour is often celebrated as a virtue, it comes at a significant cost to the health and well-being of the mothers themselves. As society evolves, it is essential to recognize and address these issues, fostering an environment where mothers can prioritize their own needs without guilt or judgment. By doing so, we can ensure not only the well-being of mothers but also the overall health and happiness of families and society at large.

*****

12. From Chaos to Calm: Mastering the Art of Peaceful Parenting

Parenting can often feel like a rollercoaster ride, filled with highs and lows, moments of pure joy, and times of utter frustration. The journey from chaos to calm in parenting is not about achieving perfection but about striving for a balanced, peaceful home where both parents and children can thrive. Peaceful parenting is a philosophy that emphasizes empathy, respect, and effective communication. This approach fosters a loving environment where children feel secure, understood, and valued, ultimately leading to more harmonious family dynamics.

"Parenting is not about raising perfect children. It's about raising humans who can navigate the world with empathy, kindness, and resilience." – L.R. Knost

Understanding Peaceful Parenting

Peaceful parenting is rooted in three main principles: connection, communication, and cooperation.

This method encourages parents to connect with their children on a deep emotional level, communicate effectively without resorting to yelling or punishment, and foster

Connection: The foundation of peaceful parenting lies in the connection between parent and child. Building a strong, secure attachment helps children feel safe and loved, which is crucial for their emotional and psychological development. This connection can be nurtured through consistent, loving interactions and by being present and attentive to your child's needs.

- **Strategies for Strengthening Connection**

Quality Time: Dedicate uninterrupted time to engage with your child. Activities such as reading, playing, or simply talking about their day can strengthen your bond.

Physical Affection: Hugs, cuddles, and gentle touches can convey love and security.

Active Listening: Pay full attention when your child speaks, showing that their thoughts and feelings are important to you.

Communication: Effective communication is vital in peaceful parenting. It involves expressing your own needs and feelings without blame or criticism and listening to your child's perspective with empathy and understanding. This two-way communication fosters a sense of respect and cooperation.

- **Strategies for Effective Communication**

Use "I" Statements: Express your feelings and needs without blaming or criticizing. For example, say, "I feel frustrated when toys are left on the floor," instead of, "You never pick up your toys."

Active Listening: Reflect back what your child says to show understanding. For example, "It sounds like you're really upset about losing your toy."

Stay Calm: Model the behaviour you want to see in your child. Keeping your cool during conflicts teaches them how to manage their emotions.

Cooperation: Encouraging cooperation rather than compliance fosters a spirit of teamwork and mutual respect. Children are more likely to cooperate when they feel their opinions and feelings are valued.

- **Strategies for Fostering Cooperation**

Offer Choices: Giving children options within acceptable boundaries helps them feel empowered and respected. For example, "Would you like to do your homework now or after dinner?"

Set Clear Expectations: Clearly communicate rules and expectations in a positive manner. Instead of saying, "Don't run," say, "Please walk."

Problem-Solve Together: Involve your child in finding solutions to problems. This teaches problem-solving skills and shows that you value their input.

- **The Benefits of Peaceful Parenting**

Adopting a peaceful parenting approach can transform family dynamics, leading to numerous benefits for both parents and children.

Emotional Regulation: Adopting a peaceful parenting approach can transform family dynamics, leading to numerous benefits for both parents and children. One of the most significant benefits is emotional regulation. Children learn to manage their emotions by observing how their parents handle conflicts and stress. When parents model healthy emotional regulation, children are taught to express their feelings constructively rather than through tantrums or aggressive behaviour. This ability to handle emotions positively impacts their interactions with others, fostering a more harmonious home environment.

Stronger Parent-Child Bond: Another key benefit is the strengthening of the parent-child bond. Peaceful parenting emphasizes connection and empathy, which nurtures a deeper, more trusting relationship. When children feel securely attached to their parents, they are more likely to open up about their feelings and experiences, knowing they will be met with understanding and support. This secure attachment is crucial for their emotional and psychological development, providing a foundation for healthy relationships throughout their lives.

Improved Behaviour: Improved behaviour is also a notable outcome of peaceful parenting. Children who feel understood and respected are more likely to cooperate and exhibit positive behaviour. This approach reduces the need for punitive measures, such as yelling or punishment, which can lead to power struggles and increased conflict. Instead, children are motivated to behave well because they feel valued and respected, leading to a more peaceful and cooperative family dynamic.

Enhanced Communication Skills: Enhanced communication skills benefit both parents and children. In a peaceful parenting framework, parents learn to communicate effectively without blame or criticism, and children learn to express themselves clearly and listen to others. These communication skills are invaluable for building healthy relationships, not just within the family but in all areas of life. Children who can articulate their thoughts and feelings and listen to others' perspectives are better equipped to navigate social interactions, resolve conflicts, and build strong, supportive relationships.

- **Practical Tips for Implementing Peaceful Parenting**

Implementing peaceful parenting requires patience, consistency, and a willingness to reflect on and adapt your parenting style. Here are some practical tips to help you on this journey.

Firstly, be mindful of your own emotions. Parenting can be incredibly challenging, often testing your patience and emotional resilience. It's essential to manage your own emotions so that you can respond calmly and effectively to your child's needs. Practising self-care is crucial; ensure you take time to recharge, whether through hobbies, exercise, or quiet time. Additionally, seek support from friends, family, or professionals when needed. By maintaining your emotional well-being, you'll be better equipped to handle parenting challenges with grace and composure.

Creating a calm environment at home is another critical aspect of peaceful parenting. A peaceful home environment significantly impacts your family's dynamics, fostering a sense of security and stability. Establishing routines can help children know what to expect, which reduces anxiety and promotes cooperation. Reducing clutter can also create a more serene atmosphere, making it easier for everyone to relax. Designating specific areas for relaxation and connection, such as a cozy reading nook or a family game area, can provide regular opportunities for bonding and unwinding together.

Practising empathy is vital in peaceful parenting. Putting yourself in your child's shoes and trying to understand their perspective can transform how you handle conflicts and daily interactions. When you respond with empathy, you validate your child's feelings, which helps de-escalate conflicts and builds a foundation of trust and security. For example, if your child is upset about something, acknowledging their feelings with statements like "I see you're really frustrated because you can't find your toy" can make them feel heard and understood, paving the way for more cooperative behaviour.

It's also essential to set realistic expectations for both yourself and your child. Recognize that perfection is unattainable, and both you and your child are learning and growing. Setting realistic expectations means being patient with your child's development and acknowledging that mistakes are part of the learning process. This patience extends to yourself as well; forgive yourself for parenting missteps and view them as opportunities for growth rather than failures.

Encouraging independence in your child is another key aspect of peaceful parenting. Allow your child to make age-appropriate decisions and take on responsibilities. This promotes a sense of autonomy and competence, which are crucial for their development. For instance, let your child choose their outfit for the day or involve them in household chores. These small decisions and tasks can significantly boost their confidence and sense of responsibility.

Focusing on positive reinforcement can also foster a more peaceful parenting approach. Acknowledge and celebrate your child's positive behaviours and efforts. Positive reinforcement, such as praise, rewards, or additional privileges, encourages the repetition of good behaviour and boosts self-esteem. When children feel appreciated and recognized for their efforts, they are more likely to continue engaging in positive behaviours.

Finally, don't hesitate to seek professional support if you find implementing peaceful parenting challenging. Parenting coaches or therapists can offer valuable insights and strategies tailored to your family's unique needs. Professional guidance can provide you with the tools and confidence to apply peaceful parenting principles effectively, ensuring a more harmonious family environment.

Overcoming Common Challenges

While the benefits of peaceful parenting are significant, the approach can also present challenges. Understanding and addressing these challenges can help you stay committed to this parenting style.

Dealing with Defiance: Children, by nature, may test boundaries and exhibit defiant behaviour as they explore their independence and understand the limits of their environment. Instead of reacting with punishment, which can often escalate the situation and create more conflict, peaceful parenting advocates for understanding the underlying reasons for such behaviour. Children might act out due to unmet needs, feelings of frustration, or a desire for attention. By addressing these root causes—such as ensuring they feel heard, respected, and valued—you can guide them towards more positive behaviours. For example, if a child is acting out because they feel ignored, spending more one-on-one time with them can help reduce their defiance.

Managing Stress: Parenting is inherently stressful, and this stress can sometimes make it challenging to maintain a calm and peaceful approach. However, managing your own stress is crucial to model the emotional regulation you want your child to learn. Incorporating stress-reduction techniques into your daily routine can be immensely helpful. Practices such as deep breathing exercises, meditation, regular physical activity, and ensuring you have time for yourself can all contribute to lowering stress levels. When you manage your stress effectively, you are better equipped to handle parenting challenges calmly and thoughtfully.

Balancing Discipline and Freedom: One of the most complex aspects of peaceful parenting is finding the right balance between setting limits and allowing freedom. Too many restrictions can stifle a child's sense of autonomy, while too much freedom can lead to a lack of structure and security. The key is to clearly communicate rules and the reasons behind them, while also giving your child opportunities to make choices and learn from their experiences. For instance, instead of enforcing a strict bedtime with no flexibility, you could offer a range of acceptable bedtimes, allowing your child to choose within that range. This approach helps children understand boundaries while also feeling a sense of control over their lives.

Consistency is Key: Consistency in your parenting approach is essential for building trust and security within the family. When children know what to expect from their parents, they feel more secure and are more likely to respond positively to guidance and rules. It's important that all caregivers are on the same page and use similar strategies to avoid confusion and mixed messages. For instance, if one parent allows certain behaviours that the other parent discourages, it can create uncertainty and lead to more behavioural issues. Regularly discussing parenting approaches and strategies with all caregivers ensures a unified front, making it easier to maintain a peaceful parenting style consistently.

Conclusion

Transitioning from chaos to calm in parenting is a journey that requires commitment, patience, and a willingness to grow alongside your child. Peaceful parenting is not about perfection but about striving for a balanced, respectful, and loving relationship with your child. By focusing on connection, effective communication, and cooperation, you can create a nurturing environment where both you and your child can thrive. Remember, the goal is not to eliminate all conflicts but to handle them in a way that strengthens your bond and fosters a positive, peaceful family dynamic.

*****

13. The Science Behind Raising Happy, Successful Kids

Raising happy and successful children is a goal many parents strive for, requiring a balanced mix of love, support, education, and guidance. While there is no single formula for success, research in psychology, education, and child development provides valuable insights into key factors that contribute to a child's well-being and achievement. From creating a loving and supportive environment to fostering a growth mindset and teaching essential social skills, understanding these elements can help parents nurture their children into well-rounded individuals. This blog explores the science behind raising happy, successful kids, offering practical tips and insights to guide parents on this rewarding journey.

"Children are not things to be molded, but are people to be unfolded." – **Jess Lair**

1. The Importance of a Loving and Supportive Environment

Emotional Security: Children need to feel safe and loved, as this emotional security forms the foundation of their development. When kids feel loved, they are more likely to explore the world around them with confidence. This sense of security comes from consistent affection, such as hugs, kind words, and active listening. It also involves setting clear boundaries and rules, which help children understand what is expected of them. Clear boundaries provide structure and stability, making children feel secure in their environment. Moreover, showing affection and listening to a child's concerns validates their feelings and builds their self-worth. Emotional security is thus a crucial element that allows children to grow into confident and well-adjusted individuals.

Positive Reinforcement: Positive reinforcement, which involves rewarding good behaviour rather than punishing bad behaviour, plays a significant role in fostering a loving and supportive environment. When parents use praise and encouragement, it motivates children to keep trying, even when things are difficult. Simple acknowledgements like "Good job!" or "I'm proud of you!" can have a big impact on a child's self-esteem and motivation. Positive reinforcement helps children understand that their efforts are valued and appreciated, which encourages them to continue striving for improvement. For instance, if a child completes their homework without being reminded, praising this effort reinforces the behaviour and makes it more likely to happen again. This approach is far more effective than focusing on mistakes, which can lead to feelings of inadequacy and decreased motivation. By consistently acknowledging and rewarding positive actions, parents can help build their children's confidence and encourage a proactive, can-do attitude.

2. The Role of Education and Learning

Encouraging Curiosity: Encouraging curiosity is essential in fostering a love for learning in children. Kids are naturally curious, and nurturing this trait helps them become lifelong learners. When parents answer their children's questions, provide books, and explore new topics together, they stimulate their minds. This curiosity-driven learning is more effective and enjoyable than forced study because it aligns with the child's natural interests and inclinations. For example, if a child shows interest in space, taking them to a planetarium or reading books about the stars can ignite a passion for science. Encouraging curiosity not only makes learning fun but also helps children develop critical thinking skills as they seek answers to their questions.

Setting High Expectations: Setting high but realistic expectations is another crucial aspect of fostering a child's educational development. When parents encourage effort and improvement rather than perfection, they help their children strive for their best. Statements like "I know you can do it if you try your best" are more effective than saying "You must get an A." This approach focuses on the process rather than the outcome, which can reduce pressure and anxiety. For instance, praising a child for their hard work on a project, regardless of the final grade, teaches them that effort is what truly counts. This not only boosts their confidence but also instils a strong work ethic and resilience, as they learn to value persistence and determination.

Fostering a Growth Mindset: Fostering a growth mindset, the belief that abilities can be developed through hard work and dedication, is vital for a child's success. Children with a growth mindset are more likely to persevere in the face of challenges because they believe they can improve through effort. Parents can promote this mindset by praising effort rather than innate talent. For example, saying "You worked really hard on that puzzle!" instead of "You're so smart!" emphasizes the importance of effort and practice. This encourages children to embrace challenges and view failures as opportunities to learn and grow. A growth mindset helps children develop resilience and a positive attitude towards learning, which are essential for overcoming obstacles and achieving long-term success. By fostering this mindset, parents can help their children become motivated, adaptable, and resilient individuals.

3. Developing Social Skills

Teaching Empathy: Empathy is the ability to understand and share the feelings of others, and it is a crucial social skill for children to develop. Teaching empathy can significantly enhance a child's ability to build strong relationships and effectively navigate various social situations. Parents play a vital role in fostering empathy by modelling kindness and understanding in their interactions with others. For instance, when parents show compassion towards someone in distress, children observe and learn the importance of caring for others. Discussing emotions openly with children is another effective strategy. By helping children label and understand their feelings, parents enable them to recognize and empathize with the emotions of others. Additionally, role-playing different scenarios can be a practical way to teach empathy. Through role-play, children can practice putting themselves in someone else's shoes and consider how they might feel and react in various situations. This hands-on approach not only reinforces the concept of empathy but also helps children develop the social skills needed to interact positively with their peers.

Encouraging Teamwork: Teamwork is an essential skill for success in life, and children can learn it through a variety of group activities. Participating in group play, team sports, and collaborative projects teaches kids how to communicate effectively, share resources, and work towards common goals. These activities provide practical experiences where children can learn the value of cooperation and the importance of each member's contribution to the team's success. Parents can further support the development of teamwork skills by encouraging their children to participate in group activities and by teaching conflict resolution skills. When conflicts arise, guiding children through the process of discussing issues calmly and finding mutually acceptable solutions helps them understand how to work harmoniously with others. By promoting teamwork, parents help children build essential social skills that will benefit them throughout their lives.

4. Physical Health and Well-being

Regular Physical Activity: Regular physical activity is vital for children's physical and mental health. Engaging in exercise helps children develop strong bones and muscles, maintain a healthy weight, and reduce stress. Activities like playing outside, participating in sports, and going on family walks are excellent ways to ensure children stay active. Making physical activity a fun and regular part of daily life can encourage children to develop lifelong healthy habits. For instance, turning exercise into a game or a family activity can make it more enjoyable and less of a chore. Parents should aim to integrate physical activity into their children's routines in ways that are engaging and enjoyable, fostering a positive attitude towards exercise.

Healthy Eating Habits: A balanced diet is crucial for a child's growth and development. Parents should provide a variety of healthy foods, including fruits, vegetables, whole grains, and lean proteins, to ensure their children receive the necessary nutrients. Teaching kids about nutrition and involving them in meal planning and preparation can help them understand the importance of healthy eating. For example, parents can explain the benefits of different foods and how they contribute to the body's overall health. By involving children in the kitchen, parents can make healthy eating an interactive and educational experience. These practices help children develop healthy eating habits that can last a lifetime, promoting their overall well-being.

Adequate Sleep: Sleep is essential for a child's physical health, emotional well-being, and cognitive development. Establishing a regular bedtime routine can help ensure children get enough sleep each night. This routine might include calming activities such as reading a book, taking a bath, and going to bed at the same time each night. Consistency in bedtime routines helps signal to the child's body that it is time to wind down and prepare for sleep. Reducing screen time before bed is also important, as the blue light emitted by screens can interfere with the body's natural sleep-wake cycle. Ensuring that children have a restful and sufficient amount of sleep supports their overall health and development, enabling them to function optimally during the day.

5. Cultivating Emotional Intelligence

Recognizing and Expressing Emotions: Cultivating emotional intelligence in children is key to their overall well-being and success. Emotional intelligence involves recognizing, understanding, and managing emotions effectively. Parents can help their children develop this skill by teaching them to identify and name their emotions. For instance, if a child is feeling angry, parents can encourage them to articulate their feelings by saying, "I'm feeling angry because..." instead of expressing their anger through negative behaviours. This practice helps children become more aware of their emotions and equips them with the language to express their feelings in a healthy and constructive manner.

Coping with Stress and Failure: Learning to cope with stress and failure is another vital component of emotional intelligence. Parents play a crucial role in modelling healthy coping strategies for their children. They can demonstrate techniques such as taking deep breaths to calm down, talking openly about their feelings, and actively seeking solutions to problems. It is also important for parents to convey that failure is a natural part of the learning process and not something to be feared. By maintaining a positive attitude towards setbacks, parents can help their children view challenges as opportunities for growth rather than as insurmountable obstacles. This perspective fosters resilience and perseverance, traits that are essential for navigating the ups and downs of life.

6. Encouraging Independence and Responsibility

Giving Age-Appropriate Responsibilities: Encouraging independence and responsibility in children is essential for their development into capable and self-reliant adults. This process begins with giving age-appropriate responsibilities, which helps children learn important life skills and gain a sense of autonomy. For younger children, tasks should be simple and manageable, such as picking up their toys or helping to set the table. These activities teach basic organizational skills and the importance of contributing to household chores. As children grow older, they can handle more complex tasks like doing their own laundry, assisting with meal preparation, or even managing a small allowance. These responsibilities not only teach practical skills but also instil a sense of accomplishment and independence.

Allowing for Natural Consequences: Another important aspect of fostering responsibility is allowing children to experience the natural consequences of their actions. This method helps them understand the link between their choices and the outcomes they produce. For instance, if a child forgets to do their homework, they might receive a lower grade. While it can be tempting for parents to shield their children from negative outcomes, experiencing these consequences teaches children the importance of responsibility and making good decisions. Parents should offer guidance and support during these times, helping their children understand what went wrong and how to avoid similar mistakes in the future.

Encouraging Problem-Solving Skills: Encouraging problem-solving skills is also crucial for developing independence and responsibility. Rather than immediately providing solutions to every challenge their children face, parents should encourage them to think critically and come up with their own solutions. This can be done by asking guiding questions such as, "What do you think you should do?" or "How can we solve this problem together?" This approach not only helps children develop critical thinking skills but also boosts their confidence in their ability to handle difficult situations. By learning to navigate problems independently, children become more resourceful and self-assured.

7. Building Strong Family Connections

Quality Time Together: Spending quality time together is crucial for strengthening family bonds and providing children with a sense of security. When families engage in activities that everyone enjoys, such as playing games, cooking meals, or going on outings, they create shared experiences that foster closeness and mutual understanding. These moments are not just about having fun but also about building a foundation of love and support. Regular family time allows children to feel valued and loved, reinforcing their emotional well-being and giving them the confidence to explore the world around them. It's during these times that children can share their thoughts, feel heard, and see their parents as a constant source of support.

Open Communication: Open communication is essential for maintaining a healthy family dynamic. It involves creating an environment where children feel comfortable expressing their thoughts and feelings without fear of judgment. Parents play a crucial role in this by actively listening, being non-judgmental, and offering support when needed. This type of communication builds trust between family members and helps children develop good communication skills. When children know they can talk openly with their parents about their worries, successes, and everyday experiences, they are more likely to seek advice and feel supported. Open communication also allows parents to understand their children better and provide guidance tailored to their individual needs.

8. Setting a Good Example

Modelling Positive Behaviour: Children learn a significant amount by observing their parents. When parents model positive behaviour, such as kindness, patience, and responsibility, they teach their children how to act in various situations. This modelling extends beyond words to actions, as children are keen observers of how their parents handle challenges, interact with others, and manage their emotions. By consistently demonstrating positive behaviour, parents set a standard for their children to emulate, helping them develop into considerate and responsible individuals. The lessons learned from watching parents can have a lasting impact, shaping children's behaviour and attitudes well into adulthood.

Demonstrating a Love for Learning: When parents show an interest in learning and self-improvement, it inspires their children to adopt a similar attitude. This can be as simple as reading books, exploring new hobbies, or discussing interesting topics around the dinner table. Demonstrating a love for learning signals to children that acquiring knowledge is valuable and enjoyable. It encourages them to be curious, ask questions, and seek out new experiences. This attitude towards learning can help children stay motivated in their education and develop a lifelong passion for discovery and growth. By making learning a visible and integral part of family life, parents can foster a positive and inquisitive mindset in their children.

Conclusion

Raising happy and successful children involves a combination of love, support, education, and guidance. By creating a nurturing environment, encouraging a love for learning, developing social skills, promoting physical health, fostering independence, cultivating emotional intelligence, building strong family connections, and setting a good example, parents can help their children thrive. Each child is unique, and there is no one-size-fits-all approach, but these principles provide a strong foundation for raising well-rounded, happy, and successful kids.

*****

14. Sibling Rivalry Solutions: Building Bonds That Last a Lifetime

Sibling rivalry is like a natural part of growing up in many families. It's when brothers and sisters feel a mix of competition and conflict with each other. This can range from small arguments over toys to bigger issues like jealousy or resentment. But here's the thing: it doesn't have to define your relationship forever. By understanding why it happens and learning how to deal with it, siblings can actually become closer and build strong bonds that last a lifetime.

"The bond that links your true family is not one of blood, but of respect and joy in each other's life." **- Richard Bach**

Understanding Sibling Rivalry

Imagine this scenario: You're happily playing with your favourite toy, and suddenly your brother or sister grabs it from your hands. Or perhaps your sister comes home with a stellar report card, and your parents shower her with praise while you feel left out. These are classic examples of sibling rivalry.

It often starts when children are quite young. They might compete for their parent's attention, which can feel scarce when there are multiple siblings in the picture. Or they might feel jealous of each other's accomplishments or privileges. As children grow older, rivalry can manifest in various ways, extending beyond toys and attention to encompass things like friends, hobbies, or even academic or extracurricular achievements.

Sibling rivalry is a complex dynamic influenced by factors like personality differences, parental attention, and societal expectations. It's important to recognize that while it's normal for siblings to have disagreements or conflicts, these can be managed and even turned into opportunities for growth and connection.

- **Why Does Sibling Rivalry Happen?**

There are many reasons why siblings might not get along:

Competition for Attention: Children naturally seek their parents' attention and affection. When parents are preoccupied with work, household chores, or other responsibilities, they may inadvertently neglect spending quality time with their children. This can lead to siblings vying for their parents' attention, resorting to behaviours like acting out or competing with each other to gain recognition. For example, a child might misbehave or excel in school to attract attention from busy parents.

Jealousy: Siblings may feel envious or resentful if they perceive their brother or sister is receiving preferential treatment from their parents. This can manifest in various ways, such as feeling overshadowed by a sibling's achievements or privileges. For instance, if one sibling consistently receives praise or rewards for their accomplishments, the other sibling may feel overlooked and harbour feelings of jealousy or inadequacy.

Personality Differences: Each child has a unique personality with distinct traits, interests, and temperaments. These differences can sometimes lead to clashes between siblings, especially if they have contrasting personalities or preferences. For instance, one sibling may be outgoing and sociable, while the other is introverted and prefers solitude. These differences in temperament and behavior can create tension or misunderstandings between siblings, leading to conflicts or competition.

Feeling Unfairness: Children have a keen sense of fairness and justice. When they perceive inequity or favoritism in their parents' treatment, it can cause feelings of resentment and bitterness. For example, if one sibling consistently receives more privileges or leniency from parents, while the other is held to stricter rules or expectations, it can breed feelings of unfairness and animosity between siblings.

Comparison: Parents, relatives, or even society at large may inadvertently contribute to sibling rivalry by comparing siblings to each other. Constant comparisons, whether in academic performance, athletic ability, or behaviour, can create pressure and foster unhealthy competition between siblings. For example, if one sibling is praised for excelling in academics, while the other is criticized for not meeting the same standards, it can lead to feelings of inadequacy and rivalry.

- **Solutions for Sibling Rivalry**

By implementing the following points one can resolve sibling rivalry:

Encourage Communication: When it comes to communication, it's essential to express your feelings openly and honestly, but in a respectful manner. If your sister keeps borrowing your clothes without asking, it might make you feel frustrated or disrespected. Instead of reacting angrily, take a moment to calm down and then approach your sister.

Choose a time when both of you are relaxed and not in the middle of any other conflicts. Start the conversation by saying something like, "Hey, I noticed you've been borrowing my clothes a lot without asking, and it's been bothering me. Can we talk about it?" By using "I" statements, you're taking ownership of your feelings without blaming your sister. Listen to her perspective too; maybe she didn't realize it was bothering you. Together, you can come up with a solution, like setting up a system where she asks before borrowing or designating certain items as off-limits.

Setting Boundaries: Setting boundaries is crucial for maintaining harmony in any relationship, including with siblings. If your brother constantly interrupts your study time, it can be very disruptive and affect your productivity. In this situation, it's important to assert yourself calmly but firmly. You might say something like, "Hey, I need quiet to concentrate on my studies. Can we agree on some quiet hours when interruptions are minimized?" By proposing a solution rather than just complaining, you're taking a proactive approach to resolving the issue. Additionally, creating a designated study area where interruptions are minimized can be helpful. This could be a specific corner of the house or even just wearing headphones to signal that you're in study mode.

Celebrating Differences: Each sibling is unique, with their own talents, interests, and passions. Celebrating these differences can help foster mutual respect and appreciation. If your sister is talented at painting while you excel in sports, take an interest in each other's hobbies. Attend her art shows or exhibitions, and genuinely praise her work. Similarly, invite her to watch your games or even participate in some sports activities together. By supporting each other's interests, you're showing that you value and respect each other as individuals, which can strengthen your bond as siblings.

Quality Time Together: Spending quality time together as a family is vital for building strong relationships with siblings. Plan activities that everyone enjoys and that encourage bonding. This could be something as simple as a family movie night where you watch a film together and share popcorn, or a picnic in the park where you play games and enjoy nature. These shared experiences create happy memories and strengthen the emotional connection between siblings. It's also an opportunity to relax and have fun together without the distractions of everyday life.

Conflict Resolution*:* Conflict is inevitable in any relationship, but it's how you handle it that matters. When you and your sibling have an argument, it's important to approach it calmly and respectfully. Take a deep breath and try to understand each other's perspectives without interrupting or getting defensive. Active listening is key here; repeat back what your sibling has said to show that you're listening and to clarify any misunderstandings. Then, work together to find a compromise that satisfies both of you. This might involve brainstorming solutions and considering each other's needs and feelings. By resolving conflicts peacefully, you not only solve the immediate problem but also strengthen your relationship by building trust and understanding.

Avoiding Favouritism: Feeling like you're being treated unfairly compared to your sibling can cause resentment and strain your relationship with them. If your parents praise your brother for his academic achievements but ignore your successes in sports, it's important to communicate how you feel. Choose a time to talk to your parents when everyone is calm and not in the midst of any conflicts. Express your feelings honestly but respectfully, using "I" statements to avoid sounding accusatory. For example, you might say, "I've been feeling a bit left out lately because it seems like you only notice when [brother] does well in school. I work really hard at my sports too, and it would mean a lot to me if you could acknowledge that." By expressing your feelings assertively but respectfully, you're opening up the lines of communication and giving your parents the opportunity to understand your perspective and make changes accordingly.

Avoiding Favouritism: Feeling like you're being treated unfairly compared to your sibling can cause resentment and strain your relationship with them. If your parents praise your brother for his academic achievements but ignore your successes in sports, it's important to communicate how you feel. Choose a time to talk to your parents when everyone is calm and not in the midst of any conflicts. Express your feelings honestly but respectfully, using "I" statements to avoid sounding accusatory. For example, you might say, "I've been feeling a bit left out lately because it seems like you only notice when [brother] does well in school. I work really hard at my sports too, and it would mean a lot to me if you could acknowledge that." By expressing your feelings assertively but respectfully, you're opening up the lines of communication and giving your parents the opportunity to understand your perspective and make changes accordingly.

Conclusion

Sibling rivalry is a common challenge in many families, but it doesn't have to define the relationship between brothers and sisters. By implementing strategies like effective communication, setting boundaries, celebrating each other's differences, spending quality time together, resolving conflicts peacefully, and avoiding favouritism, siblings can cultivate strong and lasting bonds. Recognizing that differences and disagreements are natural parts of any relationship, siblings can navigate through challenges with patience, understanding, and mutual respect, ultimately forging connections that withstand the test of time and become the foundation for lifelong friendship and support.

*****

15. Digital Parenting: Navigating the Tech Terrain with Your Kids

In an era dominated by technology, parenting has taken on a new dimension. The digital landscape, with its ever-evolving devices and platforms, poses both opportunities and challenges for parents. As children increasingly become digital natives, it's crucial for parents to embrace the role of digital guides, helping their kids navigate the online world safely and responsibly. This blog delves into the realm of digital parenting, exploring key aspects, challenges, and strategies to foster a healthy and balanced relationship between children and technology.

"The key to successful digital parenting is a harmonious blend of supervision and trust, where open communication thrives, and children are equipped with the skills to make informed decisions in the vast landscape of technology." - **Dr. Devorah Heitner**

Understanding the Digital Landscape

To effectively navigate the digital terrain with their children, parents must have a comprehensive understanding of the digital landscape. This involves staying informed about the many technologies that children encounter daily, ranging from social media platforms to educational apps. Given the dynamic nature of the online world, parents need to actively engage in ongoing learning to keep abreast of the latest trends and potential risks associated with different digital platforms.

For instance, understanding the functionalities and privacy settings of popular social media apps allows parents to guide their children on appropriate online behaviour. Likewise, being aware of the types of educational apps available enables parents to curate a selection that aligns with their child's developmental needs. This knowledge not only facilitates effective monitoring but also empowers parents to initiate informed conversations with their children about the digital tools they are using.

- **Setting Boundaries and Establishing Screen Time Rules**

One of the most pressing challenges in the digital age is managing screen time. Excessive screen time has been linked to various adverse effects on children's well-being, such as sleep disturbances, impaired social skills, and decreased physical activity. To address this, parents must establish clear and consistent screen time rules.

These rules should be tailored to the child's age, considering the developmental stage and individual needs. Collaborating with children in the rule-making process can enhance their sense of responsibility and ownership. When children actively participate in establishing guidelines, they are more likely to understand the reasoning behind the rules and adhere to them. This collaborative approach not only fosters a healthier relationship with technology but also encourages open communication between parents and children.

- **Educating Kids about Online Safety**

Digital parenting involves actively educating children about online safety. Parents should initiate age-appropriate conversations about the potential dangers that lurk on the internet, including cyberbullying, exposure to inappropriate content, and the risk of encountering online predators. Open communication is key, creating an environment where children feel comfortable discussing their online experiences and reporting any discomfort or concerns.

Implementing security measures, such as teaching children to use strong passwords and adjust privacy settings, contributes to a safer digital environment. Parents should emphasize the importance of not sharing personal information online and educate children on recognizing and responding to suspicious online behaviour. By instilling these principles, parents equip their children with the tools and knowledge needed to navigate the online world responsibly.

- **Leading by Example**

Children learn by observing the behaviour of their parents, and digital parenting is no exception. To foster responsible technology use, parents must model healthy online behaviour. This includes being mindful of their own screen time, avoiding distractions during family time, and showcasing positive online etiquette.

When parents demonstrate a balanced and mindful approach to technology, children are more likely to adopt similar habits. Creating designated tech-free times, especially during family meals and before bedtime, reinforces the importance of face-to-face interactions and promotes a healthier balance between screen time and other essential activities. By embodying the values they wish to instil in their children, parents play a pivotal role in shaping responsible digital citizens.

- **Encouraging Critical Thinking and Digital Literacy**

In the age of information, digital literacy is a fundamental skill that parents should actively promote. Beyond basic technical skills, digital literacy encompasses critical thinking and the ability to evaluate online information discerningly. Parents can help their children develop these skills by teaching them to distinguish between reliable and unreliable sources, understand the motives behind online content, and comprehend the implications of their digital footprint.

Fostering critical thinking skills empowers children to navigate the vast sea of information online confidently. Parents should engage in conversations that encourage questioning, curiosity, and thoughtful analysis of online content. By nurturing these skills, parents contribute to the development of responsible digital citizens who can navigate the digital landscape with a discerning and informed mindset.

Establishing Healthy Tech Habits

Cultivating healthy tech habits involves more than just setting screen time limits. Parents should create designated tech-free zones and times within the home. For example, bedrooms, dining areas, and family gathering spaces can be designated as tech-free zones to encourage face-to-face interactions and quality family time.

Implementing regular tech-free hours, especially during meals and before bedtime, contributes to a healthier balance between screen time and other essential activities. This not only supports children in developing a more mindful approach to technology but also strengthens family bonds. By establishing and maintaining these healthy tech habits, parents create an environment that promotes well-rounded development and positive relationships with both technology and each other.

- **Open Communication and Building Trust**

In the realm of digital parenting, trust forms the cornerstone of a healthy relationship between parents and their children. Trust is not just about allowing freedom but establishing a foundation where children feel secure discussing their online experiences openly. It's crucial for parents to convey that they are approachable and non-judgmental when it comes to technology use.

Parents should actively work towards creating an environment where children are comfortable discussing their online activities, friends, and any challenges they might be facing in the digital world. This open dialogue allows parents to gain insights into their children's online lives, making it easier to address concerns and provide timely guidance.

Regular communication is key. Parents should make a habit of checking in with their children about their online activities. This doesn't imply a lack of trust but serves as a way to stay informed about their digital experiences. By doing so, parents can offer support and guidance in real time, fostering a stronger bond built on mutual understanding.

- **Monitoring and Supervision**

While trust is crucial, especially as children grow older, supervision remains equally important, especially for younger kids. Employing monitoring tools and parental control features can aid in overseeing online activities. This balanced approach ensures a safe digital environment without stifling a child's independence or making them feel overly monitored. Parents should routinely review privacy settings on various platforms and apps their children use. This proactive measure helps in maintaining a secure online environment, preventing unauthorized access or exposure to inappropriate content. It's a collaborative effort that reinforces the importance of online safety.

Monitoring doesn't just mean surveillance; it's about identifying potential risks early on. Whether it's detecting signs of cyberbullying or recognizing inappropriate content, active supervision allows parents to intervene and guide their children appropriately.

- **Staying Informed About Emerging Technologies**

In the rapidly evolving tech landscape, staying informed is a shared responsibility. Parents and children can engage in proactive learning about emerging technologies, from virtual reality to artificial intelligence. This collaborative approach not only keeps parents in the loop but also allows children to navigate new technologies with guidance. Understanding the potential benefits and risks of emerging technologies enables parents to anticipate challenges. It allows them to establish rules and guidelines early on, ensuring a safe and controlled introduction of new tech into their children's lives. This proactive stance fosters a sense of security and preparedness.

Embracing lifelong learning is not just for children. Parents, too, should adopt a mindset of continuous education about technology. This not only enhances their ability to guide their children effectively but also showcases a positive attitude towards adapting to the ever-changing tech terrain.

Conclusion

Digital parenting is an evolving journey that requires adaptability, open communication, and a commitment to fostering a healthy relationship between children and technology. By understanding the digital landscape, setting boundaries, educating children about online safety, leading by example, and encouraging critical thinking, parents can empower their children to navigate the tech terrain responsibly. Through a combination of trust, supervision, and proactive engagement, parents can ensure that their children harness the benefits of technology while developing the skills necessary to thrive in a digital world. Ultimately, the key lies in maintaining a balanced and positive approach to technology within the family dynamic.

*****

16. 20 Time-Saving Tips for Busy Parents - Fastlane Freedom

Being a parent is a wonderful journey filled with love, joy, and countless responsibilities. However, it's no secret that being a busy parent can sometimes feel overwhelming, with never-ending to-do lists and a constant juggle of tasks. That's why finding ways to save time and streamline daily routines can be a game-changer for busy families. In this blog, we'll explore 20 simple and practical time-saving tips specifically designed for busy parents. From meal planning and delegating chores to practice mindfulness and embracing imperfection, these tips are aimed at helping parents reclaim more time for what truly matters - spending quality moments with their loved ones.

"Time is a created thing. To say 'I don't have time,' is like saying, 'I don't want to.'" - Lao Tzu

Create a Weekly Schedule:

Creating a weekly schedule is a foundational step in effective time management for busy parents. By planning out your week in advance, you can ensure that important commitments like appointments, school events, and family activities are accounted for. This helps you stay organized and reduces the likelihood of forgetting or double-booking events. With a clear schedule, you can allocate time for each task or event, allowing you to manage your time more effectively and reduce stress.

Say No to Over Commitment:

In our fast-paced world, it's easy to feel pressured to say yes to every invitation, commitment, or request that comes our way. However, constantly overcommitting ourselves can lead to burnout and leave us with little time for the things that truly matter. By learning to say no to activities and obligations that don't align with our priorities or values, we can free up more time for ourselves and our families. This means taking a step back and evaluating each opportunity that comes our way, considering whether it truly adds value to our lives and whether we have the time and energy to commit to it. Saying no can be difficult at first, but it's an essential skill for maintaining balance and focus in our busy lives.

Use a Meal Planning Service:

Using a meal planning service or app is another valuable time-saving strategy for busy parents. These tools can help you plan and prepare meals for the week ahead, taking into account factors like dietary preferences, nutritional needs, and budget constraints. By creating a meal plan in advance, you can streamline your grocery shopping process and avoid last-minute trips to the store. Additionally, meal planning can help you make healthier choices and reduce food waste by only purchasing what you need for the week.

Prep Meals in Advance:

Prepping meals in advance is a practical way to save time and simplify mealtime during the week. Spending some time on the weekend chopping vegetables, cooking grains, and portioning out snacks can make it easier to assemble meals quickly on busy weeknights. By doing the prep work ahead of time, you can minimize the time and effort required to prepare meals during the week, leaving you with more time to spend with your family.

Utilize Grocery Delivery Services:

Grocery shopping is a necessary task, but it can also be time-consuming, especially when you have a busy schedule. By taking advantage of grocery delivery services, you can save valuable time that would otherwise be spent navigating crowded aisles and waiting in long checkout lines. These services allow you to order your groceries online and have them delivered directly to your doorstep or ready for pickup at a designated time. Not only does this save time, but it also eliminates the stress and hassle of traditional grocery shopping, allowing you to focus on more important priorities.

Delegate Household Chores:

Delegating household chores is an effective way to lighten your load as a parent and foster a sense of responsibility in your children. By assigning age-appropriate tasks to your kids, you can teach them valuable life skills while also freeing up time for yourself. Whether it's folding laundry, washing dishes, or tidying up common areas, getting the whole family involved in household chores can help distribute the workload more evenly and create a sense of teamwork.

Set Up a Family Command Center:

Setting up a family command center is a practical solution for keeping everyone organized and on the same page. By creating a central location in your home where you can display important dates, schedules, and to-do lists, you can minimize last-minute scrambling and reduce the likelihood of forgetting important tasks or events. A family command center can be customized to meet your family's specific needs and preferences, whether it's a physical bulletin board or a digital calendar accessible to everyone.

Streamline Your Morning Routine:

Streamlining your morning routine can set the tone for a smoother and more productive day. By getting organized the night before—laying out clothes, packing lunches, and setting up breakfast items—you can reduce morning chaos and minimize stress. Establishing a consistent morning routine can help you start the day on the right foot and ensure that everyone in the family is ready to tackle the day ahead.

Establish Routine Bedtimes:

Adequate sleep is essential for both children and adults alike, yet it's often overlooked in our hectic lives. Establishing consistent bedtime routines for your children can help ensure they get the rest they need to thrive. This means setting a regular bedtime and following a consistent routine leading up to bedtime, such as bath time, reading a bedtime story, and winding down with calming activities. Not only does this help children fall asleep more easily, but it also gives parents some much-needed downtime in the evenings to relax and recharge. By prioritizing sleep and sticking to routine bedtimes, you can improve both your family's health and well-being.

Invest in Time-Saving Gadgets:

Investing in time-saving gadgets is another way to automate tasks and free up more time for yourself and your family. Whether it's a slow cooker for easy meal prep, a pressure cooker for quick and convenient cooking, or a robotic vacuum cleaner for hassle-free cleaning, these gadgets can help streamline household tasks and reduce the time and effort required to complete them.

Embrace Imperfection:

In a world that often glorifies perfection, it's important to remember that nobody is perfect, and that's okay. Trying to maintain unrealistic standards of perfection can be exhausting and stressful, leading to feelings of inadequacy and self-doubt. Instead, embrace imperfection in both yourself and your home. Focus on what truly matters and let go of the need to have everything perfectly organized or impeccably presented. By accepting imperfection and embracing the beauty of life's messiness, you can reduce stress and find greater joy and fulfilment in everyday moments.

Limit Screen Time:

Limiting screen time for both yourself and your children is essential for reducing distractions and fostering meaningful interactions and activities. By setting boundaries around screen time and encouraging alternative activities like reading, playing outside, or spending time together as a family, you can promote healthier habits and create a more balanced lifestyle.

Learn to Let Go:

It's easy to fall into the trap of trying to do it all, but the reality is that we only have so much time and energy to go around. Learning to let go of tasks or responsibilities that aren't essential can help us reclaim more time for the things that truly matter. Delegate tasks when possible and focus on what aligns with your priorities and values. This might mean saying no to certain commitments, outsourcing household chores, or letting go of unrealistic expectations. By learning to let go and focus on what truly matters, we can create more space in our lives for joy, fulfilment, and meaningful connections.

Batch Similar Tasks Together:

Batching similar tasks together is a time-saving strategy that can help you stay focused and avoid unnecessary interruptions. Whether it's paying bills, responding to emails, or doing laundry, grouping similar tasks allows you to streamline your workflow and maximize efficiency. By dedicating blocks of time to specific tasks, you can minimize the time spent transitioning between different activities and make better use of your time.

Practice Time Blocking:

Trying to juggle multiple tasks at once can leave us feeling overwhelmed and scattered. Instead, try practising time blocking, which involves scheduling blocks of time for specific tasks and activities throughout your day. This can help you stay focused and avoid getting overwhelmed by trying to do everything at once. Prioritize your most important tasks and allocate dedicated time blocks to work on them without interruption. By focusing on one task at a time and giving it your full attention, you can improve your productivity and make better use of your time.

Create a Family Calendar:

With busy schedules and multiple commitments, it's easy for families to become overwhelmed and disorganized. Creating a shared family calendar can help keep everyone on the same page and prevent double bookings and conflicts. This can be a physical calendar hung in a central location in your home or a digital calendar that can be accessed and updated by all family members. Include important dates, appointments, school events, and extracurricular activities to ensure that everyone knows what's happening and when. By staying organized and coordinated, you can reduce stress and create more harmony and balance in your family life.

Practice Mindful Parenting:

Practicing mindful parenting is about being present and engaged with your children when you're together. Instead of focusing on quantity, prioritize quality time spent with your kids, whether it's playing games, reading books, or simply having meaningful conversations. By being fully present in the moment and giving your children your undivided attention, you can strengthen your bond and create lasting memories together.

Prioritize Self-Care:

As parents, it's easy to neglect our own needs in favour of taking care of our families. However, self-care is essential for our overall well-being and ability to show up as our best selves for our loved ones. Make time for self-care activities that recharge your batteries and reduce stress, whether it's exercise, meditation, reading a book, or simply taking a few moments to yourself. Prioritizing self-care isn't selfish—it's necessary for maintaining balance and preventing burnout. By making self-care a priority, you can improve your physical, mental, and emotional health, allowing you to be a happier and more resilient parent.

Limit Distractions:

In today's digital age, we're constantly bombarded with distractions that can pull our attention away from what's truly important. To stay focused and productive, it's important to minimize distractions when we need to concentrate on important tasks. This means turning off notifications on our phones, setting boundaries with family members, and creating a dedicated workspace free from distractions. By limiting distractions, we can improve our efficiency and effectiveness, allowing us to accomplish more in less time and with less stress.

Celebrate Small Victories:

In the hustle and bustle of daily life, it's easy to overlook the small victories and accomplishments that happen each day. Take time to celebrate these moments, both for yourself and your children. Whether it's mastering a new skill, reaching a personal goal, or simply getting through a challenging day, every achievement deserves recognition and appreciation. By celebrating small victories, we can boost our confidence, foster a positive mindset, and cultivate gratitude for the little things in life. So don't forget to pause, reflect, and celebrate your progress along the way.

In the hustle and bustle of daily life, it's easy for busy parents to feel like there's never enough time in the day. However, by implementing the time-saving tips outlined in this article, parents can take back control of their schedules and create more space for what truly matters - family. From establishing routines and delegating tasks to prioritizing self-care and celebrating small victories, every little change adds up to make a big difference. So here's to less stress, more time, and a happier, more balanced family life. After all, the most precious thing we can give our children is our time and undivided attention.

******

17. Empowering Learning: A Parent's Guide to Home Education Success

Guiding and educating children at home by parents is crucial for several important reasons that extend far beyond the traditional classroom setting. Initially, the home environment serves as the primary and most influential learning space in a child's life, where fundamental skills and values are instilled. Parents possess a unique understanding of their children's individual needs, strengths, and challenges, enabling personalized and targeted guidance. Moreover, the home provides a secure and nurturing atmosphere conducive to experimentation, curiosity, and the cultivation of a love for learning.

"Education begins at home, and parents are the first teachers. Creating a positive learning environment fosters a love for knowledge that lasts a lifetime."

As children observe their parents actively participating in educational activities and displaying a positive attitude towards challenges, they absorb valuable lessons on perseverance, resilience, and the significance of education.

Home-based teaching also facilitates a seamless integration between formal education and daily life, offering numerous opportunities for practical learning through everyday activities. In essence, parental involvement in teaching and guiding their children at home creates a comprehensive learning experience that not only enhances academic accomplishments but also moulds well-rounded individuals prepared for the complexities of the future.

The Road Ahead

Here are the ways parents can guide and teach their children at home, fostering a supportive and enriching learning environment:

Cultivate a Positive Learning Environment

Establishing a positive learning environment at home is a foundational step in nurturing a child's educational journey. This involves intentionally creating a conducive atmosphere for learning, including a designated study space chosen to minimize distractions and equipped with the necessary tools and resources. An organized and quiet study space is essential, aiding children in focusing on their tasks and associating learning with a positive experience. To enhance this environment, parents can consider adorning the area with educational posters, charts, or their child's artwork, making it an inviting and personalized space that promotes a sense of ownership and enthusiasm for learning.

Set Achievable Goals and Expectations

Setting realistic goals and expectations is another crucial aspect of promoting a healthy learning environment at home. It requires a deep understanding of the child's abilities and tailoring expectations to their specific developmental stage. Recognizing both their strengths and areas needing improvement, parents can encourage a growth mindset by praising effort rather than solely focusing on achievements.

This approach instils in children the understanding that learning is an ongoing and evolving process, emphasizing the value of persistence and resilience in the face of challenges.

Establish Regular Routines

Creating consistent routines is a fundamental strategy to support children's learning experiences. Children thrive on predictability, and a structured daily schedule can significantly benefit their overall well-being and educational development. This routine should include consistent times for waking up, meals, play, and study periods. The predictability of such a routine creates a sense of security for children, helping them understand when it's time to focus on learning. While flexibility is important, maintaining a balance between academic and leisure activities ensures a holistic approach to a child's daily life.

Incorporate Everyday Teachable Moments

Learning isn't confined to designated study times; it extends to everyday activities. Parents can leverage these teachable moments to impart knowledge naturally and practically. Whether it's measuring ingredients during cooking, discussing the weather, or counting items while grocery shopping, these activities offer valuable opportunities for learning outside the traditional classroom setting. By incorporating education into daily life, parents can help children understand the relevance and applicability of knowledge in various contexts.

Promote Reading and Exploration

Encouraging reading and exploration is a timeless strategy for enriching a child's learning experience. Creating a home environment where books are not only celebrated but also readily accessible is key. Reading together, exploring different genres, and engaging in discussions about stories contribute to language development and stimulate imagination and creativity. Regular visits to the local library or bookstore provide opportunities for children to choose books aligned with their interests, further fuelling their passion for learning. In essence, promoting reading and exploration establishes a foundation for a lifelong love of learning and intellectual curiosity in children.

Utilize Educational Technology

In today's digital age, leveraging educational technology has become an invaluable asset in the quest for effective learning. The use of age-appropriate educational apps, online resources, and interactive learning platforms can transform mundane subjects into engaging and enjoyable experiences for children. These tools not only supplement traditional teaching methods but also cater to diverse learning styles, making education more accessible. However, it is crucial for parents to strike a balance and monitor screen time conscientiously. While technology enhances the learning process, it should not replace hands-on activities, physical play, and real-world interactions, which are essential for a well-rounded developmental experience.

Foster Critical Thinking and Problem-Solving Skills

Encouraging critical thinking and problem-solving skills is another cornerstone of effective home-based education. Parents can nurture these skills by prompting their children to ask questions, think critically, and independently tackle problems. Engaging in discussions that stimulate curiosity and challenging them to explore different perspectives fosters a mindset of continuous learning. Activities such as puzzles, board games, and science experiments not only make learning enjoyable but also provide practical applications for problem-solving. This approach empowers children to approach challenges with confidence and resilience, skills that extend far beyond the academic realm.

Cultivate Creativity through Arts and Crafts

Artistic expression through arts and crafts is a powerful avenue for cognitive development. Providing opportunities for creativity, such as drawing, painting, and crafting, not only enhances fine motor skills but also encourages self-expression and imagination. Displaying a child's creations proudly reinforces the value of their unique perspectives, fostering a sense of accomplishment and boosting their self-esteem. These artistic endeavours contribute to a well-rounded educational experience, complementing academic learning with a touch of creativity and personal expression.

Collaborate with Teachers and School

Maintaining open communication with teachers and actively collaborating with the school community is paramount for a child's holistic learning experience. By staying informed about their child's progress, strengths, and areas needing attention, parents can provide targeted support at home. Attending parent-teacher conferences, participating in school events, and engaging in the school community create a unified front, reinforcing the bridge between home and school. This collaborative approach ensures that a child receives consistent guidance and support, fostering an environment where learning can flourish both within and beyond the classroom.

Lead by Example

Leading by example is a timeless principle that holds significant weight in the context of home-based education. Children are keen observers, and they often learn more from their parents' actions than words. Demonstrating a positive attitude towards learning, embracing challenges, and showcasing a genuine love for knowledge sets a powerful example. Whether it involves reading a book, solving a puzzle, or exploring a new hobby, a parent's enthusiasm becomes a source of inspiration, motivating their child to approach learning with the same zest and curiosity. This emulation of a positive learning mindset establishes a foundation for a lifelong love of learning, proving that the most effective teaching often begins at home.

Conclusion

Home education is a fulfilling journey that requires patience, creativity, and commitment. By creating a positive learning environment, setting realistic expectations, and fostering a love for exploration and discovery, parents can lay the foundation for a lifelong love of learning in their children. Remember, the impact of a supportive home environment goes beyond academic achievements, influencing a child's overall development and shaping their future success.

*****

18. Preserving Family Culture: Strategies for Generational Bonding

In the hustle and bustle of modern life, amidst the ever-changing dynamics of society, preserving and maintaining family culture has become an increasingly relevant and essential endeavour. Family culture encompasses a multitude of aspects, including traditions, values, rituals, language, stories, and more, all of which contribute to the unique identity and cohesion of a family unit. However, with the passage of time and the influence of external factors, such as globalization and technological advancements, the continuity of family culture can face challenges. In this blog, we delve into the significance of family culture preservation and offer practical strategies for generational bonding.

"In family life, love is the oil that eases friction, the cement that binds closer together, and the music that brings harmony." **- Friedrich Nietzsche**

Understanding Family Culture

Family culture is the collective identity and shared practices that characterize a particular family unit. It encompasses both tangible elements, such as rituals and artifacts, and intangible aspects, such as beliefs and values. Family culture serves as a foundation for familial bonds, providing a sense of belonging, continuity, and identity across generations. It shapes individuals' worldview, behaviour, and relationships, influencing how family members interact with one another

Challenges in Preserving Family Culture

Family culture is facing challenges and experiencing a decline in many societies due to various factors:

- **Changing Societal Dynamics:**

Urbanization: Urbanization refers to the process of population concentration in urban areas. As more people move to cities for employment opportunities and better amenities, family structures often become geographically dispersed. Family members may find themselves living in different cities or even countries, making it challenging to maintain close-knit family bonds. The physical distance can hinder regular face-to-face interactions and limit opportunities for shared activities or celebrations. As a result, familial relationships may weaken over time, leading to a sense of disconnectedness and isolation among family members.

Nuclear Family Trend: The nuclear family, consisting of parents and their children living in the same household, has become increasingly widespread in modern society, replacing extended family structures. While nuclear families offer autonomy and privacy, they often lack the immediate support network provided by extended families. In nuclear families, the burden of caregiving, emotional support, and decision-making falls primarily on the parents, diminishing opportunities for intergenerational interaction and guidance. Consequently, family ties may become more fragmented, and children may grow up with limited exposure to the wisdom and experiences of older generations.

Dual-Income Households: In many households, both parents work outside the home to meet financial obligations and pursue career aspirations. While dual-income households provide economic stability and opportunities for personal fulfilment, they also pose challenges to family dynamics. With parents juggling work responsibilities, household chores, and childcare duties, there is often less time available for shared activities and quality bonding as a family. Traditional family rituals and routines, such as regular family meals or leisure activities, may be sacrificed in favour of work commitments, leading to a decline in familial cohesion and communication.

- **Cultural Shifts:**

Individualism: Modern societies increasingly prioritize individual autonomy and personal fulfilment, sometimes at the expense of collective family goals or traditions. The emphasis on individualism may lead family members to pursue their own interests and aspirations independently, rather than prioritizing the needs or values of the family unit as a whole. Consequently, traditional familial bonds may weaken, as individual pursuits take priority over communal harmony or cohesion.

Globalization: Globalization has facilitated cultural exchange and exposure to diverse lifestyles and values from around the world. While this cultural diversity enriches society, it can also dilute traditional family values and practices, leading to a loss of cultural identity. Families may struggle to reconcile conflicting cultural influences or adapt to changing societal norms, resulting in generational and intercultural tensions within the family unit.

- **Technological Influence:**

Digital Distractions: The proliferation of digital devices and screen-based entertainment has reshaped family dynamics, often at the expense of face-to-face communication and interpersonal connection. Prolonged screen time can detract from meaningful interactions within the family, as members become absorbed in virtual worlds or online content. Family members may retreat into their individual digital devices, diminishing opportunities for shared experiences and emotional intimacy.

Social Media: Social media platforms have revolutionized communication and connectivity but also introduced new challenges to family relationships. The curated nature of social media profiles can foster unrealistic expectations or comparisons among family members, leading to feelings of inadequacy or dissatisfaction with one's own life. Moreover, excessive use of social media may detract from real-life interactions, as individuals prioritize virtual connections over face-to-face engagement with family members.

Fragmented Attention: Constant connectivity to digital devices can result in fragmented attention within families, with members frequently multitasking or being distracted by notifications and alerts. This constant state of partial attention can undermine meaningful communication and interpersonal connection, as family members struggle to fully engage with one another. Additionally, the overuse of digital devices may lead to dependency or addiction, further exacerbating tensions within the family unit.

- **Economic Pressures:**

Financial Strain: Economic pressures, such as rising living costs, stagnant wages, and job insecurity, can place significant stress on families. To make ends meet, both parents may need to work long hours, leaving little time for family bonding or leisure activities. Financial concerns may overshadow familial relationships, as families prioritize economic stability over emotional well-being. Consequently, the lack of quality time spent together can strain family dynamics and weaken interpersonal connections.

Economic Mobility: Pursuit of career opportunities or economic mobility may require families to relocate frequently, disrupting social support networks and community ties. Relocation can uproot families from familiar environments, separating them from extended family members, friends, and community resources. The fleeting nature of modern employment may also hinder the establishment of long-term roots or stable social connections, further isolating families from meaningful support networks.

- **Modern Lifestyle:**

Busy Schedules: Hectic schedules and overscheduling of activities can leave little room for leisure time or spontaneous family interactions. In today's fast-paced world, families may find themselves caught in a perpetual cycle of work, school, extracurricular activities, and social obligations, leaving little time for relaxation or connection. As a result, family members may feel overwhelmed or exhausted, hindering their ability to nurture meaningful relationships or engage in quality bonding activities.

Stress and Burnout: High levels of stress and burnout among family members can strain relationships and impede effective communication and conflict resolution. Pressures from work, school, financial responsibilities, and societal expectations can take a toll on family dynamics, leading to tension, frustration, and emotional distance. Chronic stressors may exacerbate interpersonal conflicts or contribute to mental health issues within the family unit, further eroding familial cohesion and resilience.

Decline in Traditional Practices: Generational shifts or societal changes may lead to the abandonment of traditional family rituals, customs, or celebrations, weakening the sense of shared identity and belonging. As families modernize and adapt to changing circumstances, they may prioritize convenience, efficiency, or individual preferences over the preservation of cultural heritage or familial traditions.

Consequently, the loss of traditional practices can diminish the sense of continuity and connection within the family, as younger generations grow up without a strong link to their cultural or familial roots.

- **The Importance of Preserving Family Culture**

Identity Preservation:

Think of family culture as a big treasure chest filled with precious memories, stories, and customs passed down from our ancestors. Just like how a treasure chest holds valuable treasures, our family culture holds the essence of who we are as a family. When we make an effort to preserve our family culture, we're ensuring that our family's unique identity remains strong and vibrant. This means that the things that make our family special—our traditions, the stories of our grandparents, the way we celebrate holidays—are all kept alive. By doing this, we're making sure that our children and grandchildren will know where they come from and understand the values that have shaped our family over generations.

Bond Strengthening:

Imagine our family as a team, and each member as a player. When we do things together as a family—like having fun on holidays or taking part in special family traditions—it's like we're all working together to make our team stronger. These shared experiences create bonds between us that are stronger than anything else. They become cherished memories that we'll always hold dear, and they strengthen the love and connection between every member of our family. It's like building a sturdy bridge made of love and understanding that connects us all, making our family stronger and more resilient.

Values Transmission:

Our family culture is like a teacher that passes down important lessons and values from one generation to the next. Just like how teachers in school teach us math or science, our family culture teaches us things like respect, kindness, courage, and perseverance. These values are woven into the fabric of our family traditions and stories. When we keep our family traditions alive, we're not just having fun or celebrating special occasions—we're also passing on these valuable lessons to our children and grandchildren. This way, they learn what it means to be good people and carry forward the legacy of our family's values into the future.

- **Country Wise Example of Good Family Cultures**

When considering examples of good family cultures to adopt, it's essential to recognize that cultural practices vary significantly across countries and regions. What may work well for one family or culture may not necessarily be suitable for another. However, drawing inspiration from positive aspects of family cultures around the world can provide valuable insights for individuals seeking to enrich their own familial relationships. Here are a few country-wise examples of positive family cultures and practices:

Italy: The Italian concept of "La Famiglia" emphasizes the importance of family unity, warmth, and support. Italian families often prioritize spending quality time together, especially during meals, which serve as a central gathering point for sharing food, stories, and laughter. Family members, spanning multiple generations, maintain close bonds and provide mutual assistance in times of need. The emphasis on interconnectedness and emotional support within Italian families fosters a sense of belonging and solidarity.

Japan: In Japan, the concept of "Wa" or harmony is deeply ingrained in family relationships. Japanese families place great value on respect, cooperation, and maintaining harmonious interactions. They prioritize collective well-being over individual interests, often making decisions through consensus and considering the needs of the group. Respect for elders and ancestors is also emphasized, with traditions such as "Oseibo" (year-end gifts) and "Obon" (ancestral spirits' return) reinforcing familial ties and gratitude.

Sweden: Swedish families are known for their egalitarian values and emphasis on work-life balance. Swedish parents typically enjoy generous parental leave policies, allowing both mothers and fathers to actively participate in child-rearing and household responsibilities. The Swedish concept of "Lagom," meaning moderation or balance, encourages families to prioritize simplicity, sustainability, and equality in their daily lives. Family time is cherished, with outdoor activities and nature exploration being common pastimes.

India: Indian family culture revolves around strong familial bonds, respect for elders, and a sense of interconnectedness. Extended family structures are common, with multiple generations often living together or in close proximity. Indian families place a significant emphasis on celebrations, rituals, and festivals, which serve as occasions for strengthening familial ties and passing down cultural traditions. Respect for elders and filial piety are central tenets, with children expected to care for their parents in old age.

Brazil: Brazilian families are known for their warmth, hospitality, and emphasis on social connections. Family gatherings, known as "churrascos" (barbecues) or "rodas de samba" (samba circles), provide opportunities for relatives and friends to come together, share food, music, and conversation. Brazilian families prioritize inclusivity and emotional expression, creating an atmosphere of openness and affection. Strong community ties and support networks contribute to the resilience and well-being of Brazilian families.

Mexico: Mexican families place a strong emphasis on interconnectedness, warmth, and inclusivity. Family gatherings, known as "convivios," are common occurrences where relatives come together to share meals, stories, and traditions. Respect for elders, known as "respeto," is deeply ingrained, with children expected to show deference and care for their parents and grandparents. Mexican families also celebrate cultural events such as Dia de los Muertos (Day of the Dead) and Posadas, fostering a sense of continuity and heritage.

Norway: Norwegian families prioritize outdoor activities, nature appreciation, and a balanced lifestyle. The Norwegian concept of "friluftsliv" emphasizes the value of spending time outdoors, whether it's hiking, skiing, or simply enjoying the natural surroundings. Family outings to forests, parks, and fjords are common, promoting physical health, mental well-being, and family bonding. Norwegian families also prioritize quality time together, with evenings often reserved for shared meals and leisure activities.

South Korea: South Korean families place a strong emphasis on education, discipline, and respect for authority. The Confucian values of filial piety and loyalty are central to family dynamics, with children expected to show obedience and deference to their parents and elders. Family members often participate in collective activities such as group meals, games, and cultural outings, fostering a sense of unity and mutual support. Korean families also celebrate traditional holidays such as Seollal (Lunar New Year) and Chuseok (Harvest Festival) with elaborate rituals and ceremonies.

Kenya: Kenyan families value community, hospitality, and intergenerational wisdom. Extended family networks, known as "families of blood" and "families of choice," play a crucial role in providing social support and solidarity. Kenyan families often share resources, responsibilities, and celebrations, reinforcing bonds of kinship and reciprocity. Elders hold significant authority and are respected for their wisdom and experience, with younger generations actively involved in caregiving and decision-making processes.

France: French families prioritize the enjoyment of food, conversation, and leisure time together. Meals, particularly dinner, are considered sacred moments for family members to connect, share stories, and savour delicious cuisine. The French concept of "joie de vivre" (joy of living) emphasizes the importance of enjoying life's pleasures, whether it's through culinary experiences, cultural outings, or leisurely strolls. French families also place a premium on education and intellectual pursuits, engaging in lively discussions and debates on various topics.

- **Strategies for Maintaining Family Culture**

Family Meetings:

Schedule regular family meetings, such as weekly or monthly gatherings, to discuss important topics, make decisions together, and address any issues or concerns that may arise within the family. Create a comfortable and open environment where every family member feels heard and valued. During family meetings, encourage open communication, active listening, and respectful dialogue. Use this time to establish family goals, plan upcoming events, and allocate responsibilities. Family meetings promote transparency, problem-solving skills, and a sense of unity by fostering collaboration and shared decision-making. They provide an opportunity for family members to express their thoughts, feelings, and aspirations, strengthening familial bonds and promoting a sense of belonging.

Scheduled Family Time:

Allocating specific times during the week for family activities, such as game nights on Fridays or Sunday brunches, is crucial for fostering familial bonds. These regularly planned gatherings ensure that everyone in the family has the opportunity to participate and look forward to spending quality time together. By setting aside dedicated time for family activities, you create a sense of anticipation and excitement, reinforcing the importance of family bonding in everyone's lives. Moreover, consistent scheduling helps establish a routine that promotes family unity and strengthens relationships over time.

Multigenerational Involvement:

Encouraging interactions between different generations within the family is essential for building strong familial bonds and fostering mutual understanding. By organizing activities that appeal to everyone, such as game nights, family outings, or DIY projects, you create opportunities for shared experiences and meaningful connections. For example, grandchildren can teach grandparents how to use technology, fostering intergenerational learning and creating a sense of empowerment for both parties. Likewise, elders can share stories from their youth, passing down valuable wisdom and cultural heritage to younger generations. These interactions not only strengthen family ties but also promote empathy, respect, and appreciation for each other's perspectives.

Shared Meals:

Making family meals a priority provides a natural setting for communication, bonding, and nurturing relationships. Sitting down together to eat allows family members to share daily experiences, discuss important matters, and enjoy each other's company in a relaxed environment. Whether it's breakfast, lunch, or dinner, sharing meals as a family creates opportunities for meaningful conversations, laughter, and connection. Additionally, research has shown that regular family meals are associated with numerous benefits, including improved communication skills, better nutrition, and enhanced emotional well-being for both children and adults.

Family Projects:

Undertaking collaborative projects that engage multiple generations fosters a sense of teamwork, shared accomplishment, and mutual respect within the family. Whether it's redecorating a shared space in the house, planning a family vacation, or starting a garden, working towards a common goal strengthens familial bonds and creates lasting memories. Collaborative projects provide opportunities for family members to learn from each other, share skills and expertise, and celebrate collective achievements. Moreover, engaging in meaningful activities together promotes a sense of belonging and unity, reinforcing the notion that the family is a team that supports and cares for each other.

Cultural Immersion:

Exploring and celebrating your family's cultural heritage is a powerful way to strengthen family identity, promote cultural pride, and foster a sense of belonging. By participating in cultural events, cooking traditional meals together, or delving into genealogy research, you deepen your understanding of your roots and heritage. Embracing cultural traditions and practices not only connects you to your past but also shapes your family's values, beliefs, and identity for the future. Additionally, cultural immersion fosters appreciation for diversity, tolerance, and respect for different cultures, enriching the fabric of family life and promoting inclusivity.

Storytelling Sessions:

Set aside dedicated time, such as Sunday evenings or during family gatherings, for storytelling sessions where family members take turns sharing anecdotes, memories, and lessons learned from their lives. Encourage each family member to share a story that holds personal significance or highlights a valuable experience. This practice not only preserves family history but also strengthens emotional connections among family members. As stories are shared, listeners gain insight into each other's lives, fostering empathy, understanding, and a deeper sense of connection. Through storytelling, family members create a narrative thread that binds them together, reinforcing their shared identity and fostering a sense of belonging.

Technology-Free Time:

Designate specific periods of the day or week, such as dinnertime or weekend mornings, as "tech-free zones" where digital devices are turned off or put away. Establishing these boundaries allows family members to engage in face-to-face interaction and meaningful communication without the distractions of screens and notifications. During tech-free time, encourage activities such as board games, outdoor adventures, or simply conversing with one another. By unplugging from technology, family members can focus on building relationships, sharing experiences, and creating lasting memories together. This practice promotes mindfulness, strengthens interpersonal connections, and fosters a sense of presence and engagement within the family unit.

Volunteer Together:

Engage in community service activities as a family, such as volunteering at a local soup kitchen, participating in a charity walk, or organizing a neighbourhood clean-up. Choose volunteer opportunities that align with your family's interests and values, allowing everyone to contribute in meaningful ways. Volunteering together provides valuable opportunities for family members to work towards a common goal, fostering teamwork, cooperation, and a sense of shared purpose. Additionally, serving others cultivates empathy and compassion, as family members witness the impact of their actions on the broader community. Through volunteering, families not only make a positive difference in the lives of others but also strengthen their bonds and instil a sense of responsibility towards helping those in need.

Create Family Traditions:

Establish unique traditions that reflect your family's values, interests, and cultural background. Whether it's a yearly camping trip, a monthly movie night, or a special holiday tradition, these rituals provide opportunities for bonding, creating lasting memories, and reinforcing a sense of continuity within the family. Involve all family members in the planning and execution of traditions, allowing everyone to contribute their ideas and preferences. As traditions are passed down from generation to generation, they become woven into the fabric of family life, symbolizing shared experiences, values, and beliefs. Family traditions foster a sense of belonging and identity, creating a strong foundation for familial bonds to thrive and endure over time.

Conclusion

Preserving family culture is a labour of love that requires dedication, intentionality, and collective effort. By valuing and safeguarding our cultural heritage, we not only honour the legacy of our ancestors but also ensure a sense of belonging and identity for future generations. Through documentation, celebration, education, and adaptation, families can weave a tapestry of traditions and values that withstand the test of time, nurturing strong familial bonds and enriching the broader cultural fabric of society. As we navigate the complexities of the modern world, let us cherish and preserve the precious gift of family culture, for it is the cornerstone of our shared humanity and collective legacy.

19. Raising Independent Spirits: 20 Impactful Interactive Activities

In an era characterized by rapid change, the significance of nurturing independent and self-sufficient children holds immense importance. As parents, guardians, and educators, we bear the responsibility of providing the younger generation with the essential skills and mindset required to independently confront life's challenges. Here, we present 20 impactful interactive activities that parents can undertake with their children to promote self-sufficiency.

Cooking Together: Involve your child in meal preparation from planning to execution. Allow them to choose a recipe, make a shopping list, and assist in the kitchen. This activity not only teaches practical cooking skills but also instils a sense of responsibility and independence.

Steps:

Let your child choose a recipe they are interested in.

Create a shopping list together, considering ingredients and quantities.

Guide them through the cooking process, providing assistance when needed.

Encourage them to take ownership of the meal from start to finish.

DIY Projects: Engage in do-it-yourself (DIY) projects that require creativity and problem-solving. This can include building simple furniture, crafting, or even gardening. DIY activities promote critical thinking and boost a child's confidence in their ability to create and solve problems.

Steps:

Choose a DIY project based on your child's interests and age.

Gather necessary materials and tools.

Work together to follow instructions or come up with creative solutions.

Reflect on the project afterwards, discussing what went well and what could be improved.

Financial Planning: Teach your child basic financial skills by involving them in budgeting and saving. This activity helps them understand the value of money, make informed choices, and develop financial responsibility.

Steps:

Discuss the concept of budgeting and saving with your child.

Give them a small allowance and help them allocate funds for different purposes.

Encourage them to set a savings goal and track their progress.

Discuss spending decisions and the importance of making choices within budget constraints.

Independent Reading: Cultivate a love for reading by encouraging independent reading. Allow your child to choose their own books, fostering a sense of autonomy in their learning.

Steps:

Visit the library or bookstore together and let your child select books of interest.

Create a cosy reading space at home.

Set aside dedicated time for independent reading.

Discuss the books afterwards, encouraging your child to share their thoughts and insights.

Problem-Solving Scenarios: Create hypothetical problem-solving scenarios to challenge your child's critical thinking skills. This activity helps them develop the ability to analyse situations and come up with practical solutions.

Steps:

Present a hypothetical problem or challenge to your child.

Ask them to brainstorm potential solutions.

Discuss the pros and cons of each solution.

Encourage them to choose and implement the most suitable solution.

Setting Personal Goals: Guide your child in setting and achieving personal goals. This activity promotes self-reflection, motivation, and a sense of accomplishment.

Steps:

Discuss the importance of setting goals and how it contributes to personal growth.

Help your child identify short-term and long-term goals.

Break down larger goals into manageable steps.

Celebrate achievements and discuss any challenges faced along the way.

Community Service: Engage in community service activities together. Volunteering fosters a sense of responsibility, empathy, and a connection to the broader community.

Steps:

Explore local community service opportunities suitable for your child's age.

Discuss the importance of giving back to the community.

Volunteer together at events or organizations.

Reflect on the experience and its impact on the community.

Time Management Exercise: Teach your child the importance of time management through interactive exercises. This activity helps them prioritize tasks and allocate time efficiently.

Steps:

Create a schedule for the day with your child.

Include schoolwork, chores, free time, and other activities.

Use a timer to help them stick to allocated time slots.

Discuss the challenges and successes in managing their time effectively.

Personal Organization Challenge: Encourage your child to take charge of their personal space by organizing their room. This activity promotes a sense of ownership and the importance of maintaining a tidy and organized environment.

Steps:

Discuss the benefits of an organized space.

Provide guidance on organizing belongings and creating designated spaces.

Set a challenge to clean and organize their room within a specific timeframe.

Discuss the positive impact of an organized space on their daily life.

Decision-Making Game: Play a decision-making game that requires your child to make choices and face consequences. This interactive activity enhances their decision-making skills and understanding of cause and effect.

Steps:

Create a scenario-based game with multiple choices and outcomes.

Present dilemmas and ask your child to choose the course of action.

Discuss the consequences of their choices and alternative decisions.

Reinforce the idea that decision-making is a continuous learning process.

Nature Exploration and Survival Skills: Take your child on a nature exploration adventure and introduce them to basic survival skills. This activity not only instils a love for the outdoors but also equips them with practical knowledge.

Steps:

Plan a nature hike or camping trip.

Teach basic survival skills such as identifying edible plants, setting up a tent, and using a compass.

Discuss the importance of self-reliance in outdoor settings.

Encourage them to take an active role in planning and executing the outdoor experience.

Home Maintenance Lessons: Involve your child in basic home maintenance tasks to teach them practical skills and responsibility for their living environment.

Steps:

Include your child in minor repairs or maintenance tasks around the house.

Teach them how to use basic tools safely.

Explain the importance of regular maintenance for a comfortable living space.

Gradually assign them age-appropriate tasks, such as changing light bulbs or fixing a leaky faucet.

Mindfulness and Meditation Practices: Introduce mindfulness and meditation practices to help your child develop emotional resilience, self-awareness, and the ability to manage stress.

Steps:

Start with short mindfulness exercises, such as deep breathing or guided meditation.

Discuss the benefits of mindfulness for mental well-being.

Encourage them to practice mindfulness during challenging situations.

Share your own experiences with mindfulness to create a positive and supportive atmosphere.

Personal Reflection Journal: Initiate a personal reflection journal for your child to encourage self-reflection, goal-setting, and expressing emotions.

Steps:

Provide your child with a journal or notebook.

Encourage them to write about their experiences, feelings, and goals.

Set aside time for regular reflections and discussions based on their entries.

Support their journey of self-discovery through thoughtful conversations.

Entrepreneurial Ventures: Inspire an entrepreneurial spirit in your child by guiding them through a small business venture. This activity nurtures creativity, financial literacy, and a proactive approach to achieving goals.

Steps:

Help your child identify a simple business idea, such as a lemonade stand or handmade crafts.

Guide them in creating a basic business plan, including budgeting and pricing.

Assist with marketing and setting up their venture.

Reflect on the experience, discussing successes and areas for improvement.

Goal-Setting Board: Create a visual representation of your child's short-term and long-term goals using a goal-setting board. This activity enhances their organizational skills and provides a constant reminder of their aspirations.

Steps:

Collaboratively create a vision board with images and words representing their goals.

Discuss the steps needed to achieve each goal.

Display the board prominently in their living space as a daily reminder.

Regularly revisit and update the board to reflect evolving goals.

Inquiry-Based Learning: Encourage curiosity and independent learning by engaging in inquiry-based activities. This approach allows children to explore topics of interest, ask questions, and seek answers through research and exploration.

Steps:

Discuss your child's interests and choose a topic for inquiry.

Guide them in researching the chosen subject through books, online resources, or field trips.

Encourage them to create a presentation or report to share their findings.

Celebrate their curiosity and newfound knowledge.

Conflict Resolution Role Play: Teach your child essential conflict resolution skills by engaging in role-playing scenarios. This activity enhances their communication skills and empowers them to address conflicts independently.

Steps:

Create fictional conflict scenarios or draw from real-life situations.

Take turns playing different roles in the conflict.

Encourage your child to articulate their feelings and propose solutions.

Discuss effective conflict resolution strategies and encourage empathy.

Language Learning: Introduce your child to a new language and involve them in the learning process. Learning a language fosters cognitive skills, adaptability, and a global perspective.

Steps:

Choose a language that interests your child or has cultural significance.

Utilize language learning apps, books, or online resources.

Set language learning goals, such as mastering basic phrases or holding simple conversations.

Create a language-friendly environment at home through labels and daily interactions.

Volunteer Project Planning: Take volunteering to the next level by involving your child in planning and executing a volunteer project. This activity not only emphasizes the importance of giving back but also develops project management and leadership skills.

Steps:

Discuss potential volunteer projects or causes of interest.

Plan the project, considering logistics, resources, and goals.

Execute the project together, involving community members or organizations.

Reflect on the impact of their efforts and discuss future projects.

All these activities offer a well-rounded approach to fostering self-sufficiency in children by targeting various aspects of their development. Remember to adapt these activities to suit your child's age, interests, and individual strengths, ensuring a personalized and enriching experience.

*****

20. Crucial Role of Social and Emotional Development in Children

In the complex web of human growth, the threads of social and emotional well-being are seamlessly woven into a child's development. The journey from babyhood to teenage years is a remarkable adventure, marked not only by the growth of thinking abilities but also by the dance of feelings and social interactions. In this blog, we explore the deep importance of social and emotional development in children, looking at the crucial role it plays in shaping resilient, understanding, and socially skilled individuals.

"The greatest legacy one can pass on to one's children and grandchildren is not money or other material things accumulated in one's life, but rather a legacy of character and faith." - **Billy Graham**

Starting in Early Childhood

The roots of social and emotional development are firmly planted in the earliest stages of life. Babies, who rely on caregivers for their basic needs, are already laying the foundation for their emotional well-being. Responsive caregiving, where parents tune in to their baby's needs, creates a secure connection—a foundation for emotional development. Infants develop trust and security, forming the basis for healthy relationships later in life.

As children move through the toddler years, they start to navigate the complex world of emotions. Tantrums and outbursts are not just acts of defiance but expressions of frustration, fear, or an inability to express needs verbally. Encouraging emotional understanding at this stage, where children learn to recognize and express their feelings, sets the stage for strong emotional intelligence in the future.

- **The Important Role of Play**

Play, often seen as a simple activity, is a powerful tool for social and emotional development. Through play, children explore their emotions, develop problem-solving skills, and learn to work with others. The playground becomes a small version of society, where children experiment with social roles, communication, and solving problems.

Both structured and unstructured play are essential. Board games, sports, and activities teach children to take turns, follow rules, and work in teams—important skills in navigating social situations. Unstructured play fosters creativity and allows children to explore their emotions in a less guided environment.

- **Understanding Empathy**

Empathy, the ability to understand and share the feelings of others, is crucial for healthy social development. Children naturally have some empathy, but developing it requires intentional efforts. Encouraging children to think about others' perspectives, fostering compassion, and showing empathetic behaviour all contribute to developing this important skill.

Empathy not only helps build positive relationships but also plays a crucial role in resolving conflicts. A child with empathy is more likely to handle disagreements with understanding and kindness, setting the stage for a cooperative and harmonious society.

- **The Impact of Technology**

In the digital age, where screens dominate daily life, the influence of technology on social and emotional development cannot be ignored. While technology provides access to information, it also poses challenges. Excessive screen time can hinder face-to-face interactions, affecting the development of essential social skills.

Caregivers and educators need to find a balance, using technology mindfully and ensuring that children have enough chances for in-person social interactions. Teaching digital etiquette and fostering a healthy relationship with technology from a young age are crucial for navigating the complexities of the digital landscape.

- **Education's Role in Social and Emotional Development**

The education system is vital for shaping the social and emotional development of children. Beyond academic success, schools are places where children learn to work together, communicate, and handle various social situations. Social-emotional learning (SEL) programs are becoming more important, recognizing the need to teach skills like self-awareness, self-regulation, and building relationships.

Teachers, as important figures in a child's life, can model positive social and emotional behaviors. By creating a supportive and inclusive classroom environment, educators significantly contribute to the emotional well-being of their students, setting the stage for a positive and resilient mindset.

- **Parenting and Family Dynamics**

The family is the first and most influential social environment for a child. Parents, as primary caregivers, play a crucial role in shaping their child's social and emotional development. The quality of parent-child interactions, consistent caregiving, and the emotional atmosphere in the family all contribute to a child's sense of security and emotional well-being.

Parenting styles, from warm and responsive to strict or neglectful, significantly impact a child's socialization. A warm and responsive approach has been linked to positive social and emotional outcomes. On the other hand, overly strict or neglectful parenting may hinder a child's autonomy and emotional regulation.

Recognizing the importance of the family context, interventions that help parents create nurturing and supportive environments can have a lasting impact on a child's social and emotional development.

- **Peer Relationships and Socialization**

As children move from home to the broader social world, peer relationships become central to their development. Friendships provide a platform for learning cooperation, sharing, and solving conflicts. Peer interactions also expose children to diverse perspectives, fostering a greater understanding of the world.

However, the peer landscape has its challenges. Social dynamics, peer pressure, and the desire for acceptance can introduce stressors that impact a child's emotional well-being. Educators and parents play vital roles in guiding children through these experiences, helping them develop resilience and navigate complex social situations.

- **Cultural Influences on Social and Emotional Development**

Culture, with its various beliefs, values, and norms, shapes the socialization process of children. Cultural influences go beyond the family to include broader societal expectations. Understanding and respecting cultural diversity is crucial in fostering inclusive environments that support the social and emotional well-being of all children.

Cultural competence in parenting and education involves recognizing and respecting diverse communication styles, emotional expressions, and social norms. By embracing cultural diversity, caregivers and educators contribute to an environment where children feel valued, accepted, and understood, promoting positive social and emotional outcomes.

- **Long-Term Impact on Adult Life**

The effects of social and emotional development in childhood extend into adulthood, influencing various aspects of an individual's life. Adults who developed strong social and emotional skills in their early years tend to form healthier relationships, navigate workplace dynamics effectively, and exhibit greater overall well-being.

Conversely, individuals who faced challenges in their social and emotional development may experience difficulties in forming and maintaining relationships, managing stress, and coping with life's challenges. Recognizing the lasting impact of early experiences underscores the importance of prioritizing social and emotional development in childhood.

- **Recognizing and Addressing Challenges**

While many children navigate social and emotional development smoothly, others may face challenges that require extra support. Developmental disorders, trauma, or adverse childhood experiences can impact a child's ability to form healthy relationships and regulate their emotions.

Early identification and intervention are crucial in addressing these challenges. Collaboration between parents, educators, and mental health professionals can provide the necessary support systems to help children overcome obstacles and thrive in their social and emotional development.

- **Collaborative Efforts for Holistic Development**

Creating an environment that nurtures social and emotional development requires collaborative efforts across various areas. Parents, educators, mental health professionals, and policymakers all play important roles in supporting children on their journey to becoming socially and emotionally competent individuals.

Interdisciplinary collaborations can lead to comprehensive interventions that address various aspects of a child's life. Schools, in particular, can serve as hubs for integrating social and emotional learning into academic curricula, ensuring that these skills are not treated as separate from intellectual development but as integral components of a holistic education.

Conclusion

Social and emotional development in children is a multi-faceted journey that unfolds across various contexts and stages of life. From the early bonds formed in infancy to the complex web of peer relationships in adolescence, each experience contributes to the intricate tapestry of a child's emotional well-being.

As we navigate the challenges of the modern world, recognizing the profound impact of social and emotional development becomes crucial. It is a collective responsibility to create environments that prioritize empathy, resilience, and positive social interactions. By doing so, we pave the way for a generation of individuals who are not only academically proficient but also equipped with the social and emotional skills necessary to navigate life's complexities and contribute positively to the world around them.

*****

21. The Crucial Role of Teaching Essential Life Skills to Children

In the journey of raising children, the focus often revolves around academic achievements and extracurricular activities. While these aspects are undeniably important, there exists a realm of skills that are equally, if not more, crucial for a child's holistic development—essential life skills. These foundational abilities encompass a wide spectrum, ranging from effective communication to financial literacy and emotional intelligence. In this blog, we explore the indispensable role of teaching these life skills to children and how they serve as the building blocks for future success.

"Children need the freedom and time to play. Play is not a luxury; it is a necessity. It is through play that children at a very early age engage and interact with the world around them, laying the foundation for essential life skills." **- Kay Redfield Jamison**

Communication Skills: The Key to Connection and Understanding

Effective communication is the bedrock of success in both personal and professional spheres. It goes beyond the mere exchange of words; it's about creating meaningful connections and fostering understanding. When we teach children how to express themselves clearly, we equip them with a powerful tool for building relationships. Clear expression enables children to convey their thoughts and feelings authentically, fostering a sense of connection with others. Equally important is the skill of active listening. By teaching children to listen with intent and attention, we empower them to truly understand the perspectives of those around them. This two-way street of communication not only strengthens bonds but also promotes empathy and cooperation.

Communication skills extend into the realm of conflict resolution and negotiation. In navigating disagreements, children learn the art of finding common ground—an invaluable skill that extends far beyond the playground. These lessons in conflict resolution not only prevent conflicts from escalating but also teach children the importance of compromise and understanding, essential tools for harmonious relationships in all aspects of life. In essence, communication skills are not just about talking; they are about building bridges, fostering connections, and laying the foundation for a lifetime of successful interactions.

- **Emotional Intelligence: Nurturing Heart and Mind**

In a world that often places a premium on academic achievements, emotional intelligence emerges as a critical component of a child's development. Emotional intelligence involves recognizing and managing one's emotions, cultivating empathy for others, and learning to cope with stress effectively. These skills are not only vital for navigating the complexities of human interaction but also serve as pillars for mental well-being.

Teaching children to identify and understand their emotions is akin to providing them with a roadmap for self-discovery. By fostering emotional intelligence, we equip children with the tools to express themselves authentically and understand the emotional landscapes of those around them. This, in turn, enhances interpersonal relationships, as children learn to connect with others on a deeper, more empathetic level.

Furthermore, emotional intelligence plays a pivotal role in resilience. When faced with life's inevitable challenges, children with strong emotional intelligence are better equipped to bounce back from setbacks. They develop a positive mindset that views challenges not as insurmountable obstacles but as opportunities for growth and learning. In essence, emotional intelligence is the cornerstone of a child's ability to navigate the intricacies of human emotions, paving the way for a well-rounded, emotionally resilient individual.

Critical Thinking: Shaping Young Minds for Problem Solving

As children traverse the landscape of life, they encounter a myriad of problems, both big and small. In this journey, the ability to think critically becomes paramount. Critical thinking involves the capacity for problem-solving, decision-making, and logical reasoning.

Encouraging children to approach challenges with creativity unlocks their potential for innovative thinking. By cultivating a mindset that values analysing situations thoughtfully, we lay the foundation for a generation capable of navigating an ever-changing world. These skills extend beyond the academic realm; they empower individuals to confront real-world issues with confidence and adaptability.

Critical thinking not only enhances academic performance but also fosters adaptability in the face of future uncertainties. In a world that constantly evolves, the ability to think critically positions children to meet challenges head-on, equipped with the skills needed to find innovative solutions. Critical thinking is more than an academic pursuit;

it's a skill set that shapes young minds, preparing them to tackle the complexities of life with resilience and ingenuity.

Time Management: A Lifelong Skill for Success

Time, once spent, is irreplaceable. Teaching children the importance of managing their time effectively is akin to providing them with a lifelong gift. From prioritizing tasks to setting achievable goals, time management skills empower children to take control of their responsibilities and accomplishments.

In the academic realm, effective time management is synonymous with academic success. When children learn to allocate their time wisely, they enhance their ability to focus on tasks, leading to improved performance. This extends into their personal and professional lives, where the ability to prioritize tasks becomes a cornerstone of success.

Understanding the value of time instils a sense of discipline and responsibility. When children grasp the finite nature of time, they become more mindful of how they allocate their most precious resources. This awareness lays the groundwork for success in academic pursuits, professional endeavours, and personal goals. Time management is not just about scheduling; it's about instilling a sense of discipline that propels children toward success in every facet of life.

Resilience: Bouncing Back from Life's Hurdles

Life is a journey filled with ups and downs, and resilience emerges as the key to bouncing back from setbacks. Teaching children to embrace failure as a part of the learning process, adapt to changes, and maintain a positive mindset in the face of adversity lays the groundwork for a resilient attitude. Resilience is more than just weathering life's storms; it's about thriving in the midst of challenges. When children learn to view setbacks not as insurmountable obstacles but as opportunities for growth, they develop a mindset that propels them forward.

These skills contribute significantly to mental and emotional well-being. Resilient individuals possess the ability to cope with stress effectively, managing the inevitable pressures of life with grace and poise. By instilling resilience, we provide children with the tools to navigate the complexities of the human experience. Resilience is not just about enduring challenges; it's about empowering children to face life's hurdles with a spirit of optimism, resilience, and unwavering determination.

Financial Literacy: Equipping Children for Financial Independence

In today's intricate financial landscape, imparting financial literacy to children is paramount. The fundamental concepts of budgeting, understanding the value of money, and cultivating a habit of saving are pivotal in laying the groundwork for responsible financial decision-making. By providing children with these skills, we empower them to confidently navigate the intricate world of personal finance. Budgeting instils a sense of fiscal responsibility, helping children grasp the importance of managing their resources wisely. Understanding the value of money goes beyond its face value, encompassing concepts like earning, spending, and saving.

Cultivating a habit of saving is a cornerstone of financial independence. Teaching children the significance of setting aside a portion of their resources for the future instils a sense of foresight and planning. These skills not only contribute to their immediate financial well-being but also foster a long-term mindset that is crucial for future success. Ultimately, by instilling financial literacy in children, we equip them with the tools to make informed financial decisions, promoting a sense of independence and setting the stage for a secure financial future.

Self-Care and Healthy Living: Nourishing the Body and Mind

In the pursuit of a fulfilling life, the foundation lies in the dual pillars of physical and mental well-being. Teaching children the importance of personal hygiene, healthy eating habits, and regular exercise is akin to laying the groundwork for a lifetime of self-care. Personal hygiene goes beyond cleanliness; it instils a sense of self-respect and responsibility for one's well-being. Cultivating healthy eating habits imparts the knowledge of nutrition, promoting not just physical health but also cognitive function and emotional well-being.

Regular exercise is a cornerstone of a healthy lifestyle, contributing to physical fitness and mental clarity. By instilling these habits early on, we contribute to the development of a robust foundation for overall well-being. These practices, when integrated into a child's daily routine, become ingrained in their lifestyle choices, setting the stage for a healthier and more fulfilling life. In essence, by emphasizing self-care and healthy living, we empower children to prioritize their well-being, fostering habits that will serve them throughout their lives.

Social Skills: Building Bridges and Breaking Barriers

As inherently social beings, the ability to forge and sustain relationships is a fundamental aspect of human life. Teaching children essential social skills, including effective communication, teamwork, and empathy, goes beyond mere interpersonal dynamics; it lays the foundation for positive connections with peers and adults alike. Effective communication ensures that children can express themselves clearly and understand others empathetically, fostering harmonious social interactions.

The emphasis on teamwork instils the value of collaboration, a skill that extends beyond the playground into academic and professional settings. Through collaboration, children learn the importance of mutual respect, shared goals, and collective achievement. Empathy, a cornerstone of social intelligence, enables children to understand and connect with others on a deeper level, contributing to a compassionate and interconnected community. In essence, teaching social skills not only contributes to a harmonious social environment but also equips children with the tools for successful collaboration, both in their academic journey and future professional endeavours.

Digital Literacy: Navigating the Digital Landscape Safely

In the age of rapid technological advancement, navigating the online world is an essential skill for children. Teaching them responsible technology use, online safety, and digital etiquette is crucial for their overall well-being. Responsible technology use involves imparting an understanding of the potential benefits and risks associated with digital tools. By educating children on the importance of discernment and moderation in their digital interactions, we help them harness the advantages of technology while mitigating potential pitfalls.

Online safety is a critical component of digital literacy, encompassing knowledge about privacy protection, secure online practices, and the potential consequences of online behaviour. Digital etiquette, or "netiquette," involves teaching children how to communicate respectfully and responsibly in online environments. By instilling these digital literacy skills, we empower children to navigate the digital landscape safely, fostering a sense of responsibility and awareness as they engage with technology. Ultimately, the goal is to contribute to the development of responsible digital citizens who can leverage technology for positive purposes while safeguarding their well-being.

Self-Advocacy: Empowering Children to Speak Up

The ability to advocate for oneself is a foundational skill that empowers children to express their needs, opinions, and boundaries confidently. Teaching assertiveness involves providing children with the tools to communicate effectively without being passive or aggressive. By encouraging them to express their thoughts and preferences clearly, we foster a sense of self-assurance and autonomy.

Understanding the importance of seeking help when needed is a crucial aspect of self-advocacy. By normalizing the idea that asking for assistance is a strength, not a weakness, we equip children with the humility to recognize when they require support. Additionally, instilling a comprehension of personal rights and responsibilities contributes to the development of ethical decision-making and a sense of accountability.

These self-advocacy skills are not only invaluable in academic settings but also extend to personal relationships and professional endeavours. In educational environments, self-advocacy enables children to actively participate in their learning journey, expressing their unique needs and learning styles. In personal relationships, it facilitates effective communication and boundary-setting. In the professional realm, self-advocacy is a cornerstone of career success, empowering individuals to navigate challenges and pursue opportunities with confidence. In essence, by empowering children to speak up, we contribute to their overall development as assertive, self-aware, and resilient individuals.

Creativity: Unlocking the Power of Imagination

Creativity is a dynamic force that propels innovation and problem-solving, making it an indispensable skill for children. By encouraging them to transcend boundaries, approach challenges with imaginative solutions, and express their creativity, we cultivate a love for learning and an innovative mindset. These skills extend beyond traditional artistic endeavours, permeating various facets of life.

In the realm of problem-solving, creative thinking allows children to devise unconventional solutions, fostering adaptability and resilience. When faced with challenges, those who can think creatively are better equipped to navigate uncertainty, embracing a mindset that views obstacles as opportunities for innovation. This creative approach to problem-solving lays the groundwork for future success in academic, professional, and personal spheres.

Moreover, creativity enhances a child's ability to communicate ideas effectively. Whether through writing, visual arts, or other forms of expression, fostering creativity nurtures effective communication skills. This ability to convey thoughts imaginatively not only enriches personal expression but also promotes a deeper understanding of complex concepts. Creativity is a versatile skill that empowers children to think critically, communicate effectively, and approach challenges with a sense of innovation. By unlocking the power of imagination, we equip them with the tools needed to thrive in a world that values adaptability and inventive thinking.

Basic Cooking and Home Management: Life Skills for Independence

As children transition into adulthood, the acquisition of fundamental life skills becomes paramount for fostering independence. Basic cooking and home management skills are integral components of this journey, preparing them for the responsibilities associated with maintaining a living space and achieving self-sufficiency.

Teaching children simple cooking skills not only equips them with the ability to prepare nutritious meals but also instils an appreciation for the importance of a healthy lifestyle.

Understanding the basics of cleanliness and organization contributes to the creation of a conducive living environment, promoting overall well-being. Basic household chores, often overlooked, play a crucial role in cultivating a sense of responsibility and accountability. Through these tasks, children learn the importance of contributing to shared spaces, developing habits that will serve them well in communal living situations and future relationships.

By imparting these life skills, we empower children to navigate the practicalities of daily life with confidence. From planning meals to organizing living spaces, these skills form the foundation for an independent and well-rounded adult. Ultimately, the teaching of basic cooking and home management is an investment in their future, preparing them for the challenges and responsibilities that come with adulthood.

Organization Skills: A Key to Success in Any Endeavor

The ability to organize and manage tasks is a cornerstone of success in both personal and professional endeavours. Teaching children organizational skills is akin to providing them with a toolkit for efficiency and productivity, essential qualities that contribute to their overall success. Keeping track of belongings is not merely about tidiness; it is a habit that reflects order and responsibility. By instilling this practice, children develop a sense of ownership over their possessions and reduce the likelihood of disorganization and stress.

The skill of planning and organizing tasks extends beyond the immediate benefits of time management. It involves breaking down complex goals into manageable steps, and fostering a strategic approach to problem-solving and goal achievement. This skill set, when honed early on, translates into academic success and later into a successful career.

Maintaining a tidy living space contributes to a positive and conducive environment for both work and relaxation. Children who grow up with an appreciation for cleanliness and organization are more likely to carry these habits into adulthood, positively impacting their overall quality of life. Organization skills are not only practical but also transformative. They lay the groundwork for a disciplined and goal-oriented mindset that sets the stage for success in any endeavour, whether academic, professional, or personal.

Empathy and Cultural Competence: Fostering Global Citizens

In an increasingly interconnected world characterized by diversity, fostering empathy and cultural competence is imperative. Teaching children to understand and appreciate different cultures, respect differences, and develop a global mindset is an investment in their ability to thrive as compassionate and open-minded individuals.

Empathy, the ability to understand and share the feelings of others, is a foundational skill for building meaningful relationships. By cultivating empathy, children develop the capacity to connect with people from diverse backgrounds, fostering a sense of unity and shared humanity. Cultural competence goes beyond tolerance; it involves actively seeking to understand and appreciate the richness of different cultures. By exposing children to diverse perspectives and traditions, we prepare them to navigate a globalized world with respect and an open heart.

A global mindset is an essential component of success in various fields, from business to diplomacy. Children who grow up with an understanding of global interdependence are better equipped to collaborate and communicate effectively on an international scale, contributing to the creation of a more interconnected and harmonious world. Fostering empathy and cultural competence in children is not only a moral imperative but also a strategic investment in their future success. By developing these skills, we contribute to the creation of compassionate, open-minded, and globally aware citizens who are well-prepared to navigate the complexities of our diverse world.

Environmental Awareness: Stewardship for a Sustainable Future

As stewards of the planet, instilling environmental awareness in children is a critical undertaking. Teaching them the importance of environmental conservation, practising sustainable habits, and understanding the impact of individual actions on the planet lays the foundation for the development of environmentally conscious citizens. Environmental conservation involves instilling a sense of responsibility for the planet and its resources. By teaching children, the importance of reducing waste, conserving energy, and protecting natural habitats, we contribute to the creation of a generation that actively participates in preserving the Earth for future generations.

Practising sustainable habits extends beyond the immediate benefits of environmental conservation; it also instils a mindset of responsibility and resourcefulness. Children who grow up with an awareness of sustainable practices are more likely to make choices that prioritize long-term well-being over short-term convenience. Understanding the impact of individual actions on the planet is a key aspect of environmental literacy. By educating children about the interconnectedness of ecosystems and the consequences of environmental degradation, we empower them to make informed choices that contribute to a sustainable and thriving future.

Conclusion

In conclusion, the crucial role of teaching essential life skills to children cannot be overstated. These skills serve as the building blocks for a successful and fulfilling life, contributing to personal development, interpersonal relationships, and societal well-being. As parents, educators, and community members, it is our collective responsibility to prioritize the holistic development of children, equipping them with the tools they need to navigate the complexities of the modern world. By investing in the development of essential life skills, we pave the way for a generation of individuals who are not only academically proficient but also emotionally intelligent, socially adept, and well-prepared for the challenges and opportunities that lie ahead.

*****

22. Empathy Starts at Home: Teaching Your Child the Gift of Kindness

In a world that often seems fast-paced and competitive, fostering empathy in children becomes a crucial aspect of their emotional and social development. Empathy, the ability to understand and share the feelings of others, is a fundamental skill that can significantly impact a child's relationships and overall well-being. While schools play a role in shaping a child's character, the foundation of empathy is laid at home. This blog explores the importance of empathy, its benefits, and practical ways parents can nurture this essential quality in their children.

"In the garden of humanity, empathy is the seed we plant at home, and kindness is the flower that blooms, spreading its fragrance far and wide." **- Amit Ray**

Understanding Empathy

Empathy is more than just a buzzword; it is a cornerstone of healthy relationships and emotional intelligence. It involves the ability to recognize and respond to the feelings of others, fostering a sense of connection and understanding. There are three main types of empathy: cognitive empathy, emotional empathy, and compassionate empathy.

Cognitive Empathy: This refers to the ability to understand another person's perspective or point of view. It involves putting oneself in someone else's shoes and seeing a situation from their vantage point.

Emotional Empathy: This involves sharing and understanding the emotions of others. Children with emotional empathy can connect with someone else's joy or sadness on a deep emotional level.

Compassionate Empathy: The highest form of empathy, compassionate empathy, not only involves understanding and sharing another person's feelings but also motivates individuals to take positive actions to help alleviate someone's pain or suffering.

- **The Benefits of Empathy for Children**

Teaching empathy to children goes beyond instilling good manners; it lays the groundwork for a compassionate and considerate society. The benefits of nurturing empathy in children are vast and have a lasting impact on various aspects of their lives.

Enhanced Social Skills: The development of enhanced social skills is one of the primary benefits of nurturing empathy in children. Empathetic children naturally gravitate towards stronger interpersonal relationships. Understanding and sharing the feelings of others equip them with the ability to communicate more effectively. They become adept at reading social cues, accurately interpreting emotions, and responding in a considerate manner. This proficiency in social dynamics not only helps them form deeper connections with their peers but also fosters a positive social environment. Empathetic children are more likely to engage in cooperative play, collaborative learning, and inclusive activities, which contribute to a harmonious and supportive community.

Reduced Aggression: Empathy acts as a natural deterrent to aggressive or harmful behaviour in children. When children understand the impact of their actions on others, they are less inclined to engage in behaviours that could cause harm or distress. By recognizing and sharing the feelings of those around them, empathetic children develop a heightened awareness of the consequences of their actions. This awareness serves as a powerful motivator for making choices that contribute positively to their social environment. As a result, instances of bullying, teasing, or other aggressive behaviours are significantly reduced, creating a safer and more inclusive atmosphere for all children.

Improved Emotional Regulation: Empathy plays a crucial role in helping children recognize and manage their own emotions effectively. By understanding the emotions of others, empathetic children develop a nuanced understanding of different emotional states. This increased emotional intelligence empowers them to navigate their own feelings in a healthy and constructive manner. Rather than reacting impulsively to emotional stimuli, empathetic children learn to pause, reflect, and choose appropriate responses. This heightened emotional regulation contributes to their overall well-being and resilience, enabling them to cope more effectively with the challenges and stressors they may encounter.

Better Problem-Solving Skills: Empathetic children excel at problem-solving due to their ability to consider various perspectives. In both academic and real-world scenarios, this skill proves invaluable. When faced with a challenge, empathetic children naturally seek to understand the viewpoints and concerns of others involved. This collaborative approach to problem-solving promotes creativity and innovation. By considering multiple perspectives, empathetic children can arrive at solutions that take into account the diverse needs and interests of those involved. This not only enhances their academic performance but also prepares them for success in various professional and personal contexts where effective problem-solving is essential.

Increased Self-Esteem: Experiencing the positive impact of their actions on others contributes significantly to the development of a child's self-esteem. Acts of kindness and empathy create a sense of accomplishment and fulfilment in empathetic children. As they witness the positive consequences of their considerate behaviour, they gain confidence in their ability to make a difference in the lives of others. This positive reinforcement fosters a healthy sense of self-worth and encourages children to continue engaging in empathetic actions. Ultimately, the reciprocal nature of empathy enhances a child's perception of their own value and the positive influence they can have on their social environment.

Nurturing Stronger Relationships: Empathy forms the basis of strong, meaningful relationships throughout a child's life. Children who understand and respect the feelings of others are more likely to build trust and rapport with their peers, family members, and, later in life, with colleagues and romantic partners. Empathetic children are skilled at recognizing the needs of those around them, fostering a sense of connection and understanding. This ability to empathize creates a supportive and nurturing foundation for relationships, where open communication, mutual respect, and shared understanding thrive. As children carry these empathetic qualities into adulthood, they contribute to the creation of compassionate communities and enriching interpersonal connections.

- **Nurturing Empathy at Home**

Now that we understand the importance of empathy, let's explore practical ways parents can foster this essential quality in their children within the confines of the home environment.

Be a Role Model: Children often emulate the behaviour of their parents. By consistently demonstrating empathy in your interactions, you provide a powerful example for your child. Whether it's expressing understanding when they face challenges or being considerate in your dealings with others, your actions become a living lesson in empathy. Share stories about your own experiences where empathy made a difference, and explain the thought process behind your considerate actions. This helps children understand the practical aspects of empathy in real-life situations.

Encourage Emotional Expression: Creating a safe space for your child to express emotions freely fosters emotional intelligence, a critical component of empathy. When children feel that their feelings are acknowledged and respected, they are more likely to extend the same courtesy to others. Initiate open conversations about emotions and encourage your child to describe how they feel. Provide language for emotions they may struggle to express, helping them build a nuanced emotional vocabulary.

Practice Active Listening: Active listening involves not just hearing but truly understanding what others are saying. Teaching your child this skill enhances their cognitive empathy by helping them comprehend different perspectives and emotions. During conversations, model active listening by maintaining eye contact, nodding, and responding thoughtfully to what your child says. Encourage them to ask follow-up questions to show genuine interest in others' experiences.

Read Books on Empathy: Stories have a unique ability to evoke empathy. By choosing age-appropriate books that highlight empathy and kindness, you expose your child to different perspectives and emotions, fostering a deeper understanding of the human experience. Discuss the characters' emotions, motivations, and actions in the stories you read together. Relate the events in the books to real-life situations, encouraging your child to consider how they would react in similar circumstances.

Volunteer Together: Engaging in volunteer activities as a family provides practical, hands-on lessons in compassionate empathy. Working together to help those less fortunate not only instils a sense of gratitude but also deepens understanding of the struggles others may face. Choose volunteer activities that align with your child's interests. Discuss the impact of your actions and highlight the positive change that can result from collective efforts, reinforcing the value of empathy in making a difference.

Discuss Real-Life Scenarios: Everyday situations offer opportunities to discuss and develop empathy. By prompting your child to consider their own and others' feelings in various scenarios, you nurture their cognitive empathy. Bring up situations from daily life or current events and ask open-ended questions. Encourage your child to explore different perspectives, fostering a habit of considering others' feelings in their decision-making process.

Set Expectations for Behaviour: Establishing clear expectations for empathetic behaviour at home reinforces the importance of kindness, sharing, and consideration for others. Consistency in these expectations helps in internalizing these values. Clearly communicate your family values regarding empathy. Reinforce positive behaviour through praise and acknowledgment while addressing lapses with constructive discussions rather than punitive measures.

Foster a Sense of Responsibility: Encouraging your child to take responsibility for their actions helps them understand the impact of their behaviour on others. This sense of accountability is foundational for the development of compassionate empathy. Discuss the consequences of actions, both positive and negative. Encourage your child to reflect on how their behaviour may have influenced others' feelings, fostering an awareness of the interconnectedness of emotions.

Emphasize Perspective-Taking: Developing perspective-taking skills is crucial for empathy. By encouraging your child to consider different viewpoints through activities like role-playing or discussing hypothetical scenarios, you enhance their ability to understand others' feelings. Engage in role-playing activities where you and your child take on different roles to understand varied perspectives. Discuss how people may feel in different situations, encouraging empathy through imagination and understanding.

Provide Constructive Feedback: Positive reinforcement for empathetic behaviour reinforces its importance, while constructive feedback for mistakes helps in learning and growth without instilling fear. Acknowledge and praise your child when they display empathy. When mistakes occur, use these instances as teaching moments. Discuss alternative actions and emphasize the impact of their choices on others, guiding them toward more empathetic behaviour.

Conclusion

Empathy is a gift that keeps on giving, shaping not only the individual but also the world they inhabit. By instilling the value of empathy at home, parents contribute to the creation of a kinder, more compassionate society. In teaching children the art of understanding and sharing the feelings of others, parents equip them with the tools necessary to navigate the complexities of relationships and to make positive contributions to the world around them. Empathy truly starts at home, and the lessons learned within the family environment lay the foundation for a future filled with kindness and understanding.

*****

23. A Balanced Approach: Nurturing Children Without Overscheduling

In the fast-paced world we live in, parents often find themselves caught in the struggle to provide their children with enriching experiences while avoiding the pitfalls of overscheduling. The pressure to enrol children in numerous extracurricular activities can be overwhelming, yet purposeful parents are increasingly recognizing the importance of a balanced approach to child development. This blog explores the significance of nurturing children without succumbing to the threats of overscheduling, focusing on the benefits of a mindful and well-rounded parenting approach.

"Childhood is a journey, not a race. Let's savour the moments, nurture their passions, and provide the space for unstructured play—the building blocks of a well-balanced and fulfilling life."

Understanding Overscheduling

Overscheduling is a phenomenon where children find themselves engrossed in a multitude of organized activities, often to the detriment of unstructured play, relaxation, and essential family bonding. The desire to equip children with every conceivable advantage can inadvertently lead to negative consequences, impacting their physical and mental well-being. To truly grasp the implications of overscheduling, it is crucial to delve into the motivations behind this trend and explore how a balanced approach can better serve the overall development of the child.

In many cases, the drive for overscheduling arises from a well-intentioned desire to provide children with opportunities for enrichment and success. Parents, influenced by societal pressures and a competitive educational landscape, may believe that filling a child's schedule with a myriad of activities will set them on a trajectory toward excellence. However, this quest for excellence can come at a significant cost.

- **Balanced Development**

A fundamental principle of nurturing children without succumbing to overscheduling is the emphasis on balanced development. Purposeful parents recognize that a child's growth extends beyond academic achievements or the acquisition of specific skills. A well-rounded approach encompasses physical, emotional, social, and intellectual development. By steering away from an excessive focus on a single area, parents can foster a holistic approach to learning that prepares children for the multifaceted challenges of life.

In the pursuit of balance, parents may encourage their children to explore a variety of activities, allowing them to discover their strengths and interests. This approach not only promotes a more comprehensive skill set but also helps children develop a sense of versatility and adaptability, essential qualities for success in diverse environments.

- **Quality Over Quantity**

Rather than overwhelming a child's schedule with an abundance of activities, purposeful parents prioritize quality over quantity. Selecting a few well-chosen activities that align with a child's interests and aptitudes facilitates a more profound and meaningful engagement. This strategic approach not only guards against burnout but also instils in children a sense of passion and dedication for the activities they choose. This early exposure to the value of quality over quantity lays the foundation for a mindset of lifelong learning.

Parents who adopt the quality-over-quantity mindset also recognize that the richness of an experience is often more important than the sheer volume of activities. Whether it's mastering a musical instrument, engaging in a team sport, or participating in an art class, the depth of understanding and commitment to a chosen pursuit can foster valuable life skills such as discipline, perseverance, and time management.

- **Time for Unstructured Play**

Unstructured play is a vital component of childhood development that contributes to creativity, problem-solving skills, and social competence. Purposeful parents understand the value of allowing their children time for spontaneous, imaginative play that is not directed or supervised by adults. In the absence of a rigid schedule, children have the freedom to explore their interests, develop their imagination, and engage in activities driven by their intrinsic curiosity.

Unstructured play encourages the development of independence as children learn to make decisions, solve problems, and entertain themselves without constant adult guidance. These experiences contribute to the formation of crucial life skills, including self-regulation, creativity, and the ability to navigate social interactions—all of which are integral to a child's overall growth.

- **Family Time and Shared Experiences**

In the midst of the hustle and bustle of contemporary life, purposeful parents recognize the paramount importance of prioritizing family time and fostering shared experiences. In a world where time seems to slip away quickly, these parents intentionally carve out moments for their families to connect and bond. Whether through weekend outings, shared meals, or simple evenings of storytelling, these shared experiences go beyond mere recreational activities—they become the building blocks of a strong family foundation.

Weekend outings provide an opportunity for families to escape the routine and explore together. Whether it's a visit to a local park, a nature hike, or a cultural trip, purposeful parents understand that these shared adventures create lasting memories. The laughter, conversations, and shared discoveries during these outings contribute significantly to the fabric of family life, reinforcing the emotional ties that bind family members.

Shared meals hold a special place in purposeful parenting. Gathering around the table provides an intimate setting for family members to share their day, discuss experiences, and simply enjoy each other's company. The act of sharing a meal transcends the nutritional aspect; it becomes a communal experience that fosters communication, connection, and a sense of unity.

Simple evenings of storytelling or engaging in leisure activities at home are equally valuable. Purposeful parents recognize that the quality of time spent together matters more than the quantity. Whether it's playing board games, reading books, or engaging in creative projects, these shared moments contribute to the development of a supportive and nurturing family environment.

The importance of these shared experiences lies in their ability to strengthen familial bonds and contribute to a child's sense of belonging. In a world where external influences can often pull family members in different directions, purposeful parents deliberately create a space for shared activities that reinforce the family unit as a source of support, love, and security.

- **Avoiding Burnout and Stress**

Children subjected to overscheduling can experience a range of negative effects, including burnout, stress, and anxiety. Purposeful parents are keenly aware of the potential pitfalls of excessive demands on their children's time and energy. They actively work to protect their children from unnecessary pressure, recognizing that a child's well-being extends beyond academic or extracurricular achievements.

Recognizing the signs of stress in children is a crucial aspect of purposeful parenting. Changes in behaviour, mood swings, or a decline in academic performance may indicate that a child is overwhelmed. Purposeful parents remain vigilant, staying attuned to their child's emotional and physical well-being. This awareness enables them to make informed decisions about their child's schedule, intervening when necessary to promote a healthier and more positive overall experience.

The active avoidance of excessive demands doesn't imply a lack of ambition or drive; rather, purposeful parents understand the delicate balance between pushing a child to excel and allowing them the necessary space to grow and explore. By maintaining this equilibrium, purposeful parents contribute to their child's overall resilience and ability to cope with challenges.

- **Respecting Individual Needs**

Every child is a unique individual with distinct needs, interests, and energy levels. Purposeful parents invest time and effort in understanding their child's personality, preferences, and limits. This personalized approach ensures that the activities in which a child engages align with their strengths and interests, promoting a sense of fulfilment and accomplishment.

This respect for individual needs goes beyond the recognition of academic or extracurricular strengths; it encompasses a holistic understanding of a child's emotional and social well-being. Purposeful parents create an environment where their children feel seen and understood, fostering a sense of security and self-acceptance. Tailoring activities to align with a child's strengths not only enhances their sense of accomplishment but also contributes to the development of a positive self-image. Purposeful parents understand that a child who feels supported and valued is more likely to embrace challenges and approach new experiences with confidence.

- **Teaching Essential Life Skills**

A balanced approach to nurturing children involves more than academic or extracurricular achievements—it extends to the intentional teaching of essential life skills. Purposeful parents view a well-structured schedule as a tool for imparting these skills gradually, preparing their children for the demands of adulthood.

Time management and prioritization are among the critical life skills purposeful parents aim to instil. By involving children in the decision-making process regarding their activities, parents empower them to take responsibility for their time and commitments. This gradual introduction to time management not only helps children develop organizational skills but also instils a sense of accountability.

The decision-making process becomes a valuable learning experience, teaching children to weigh priorities and make informed choices. Purposeful parents understand that these skills lay the groundwork for future success, both academically and in their professional lives.

- **Promoting Independence and Autonomy**

Overscheduling can inadvertently hinder a child's opportunities to explore personal interests and develop a sense of independence. Purposeful parents actively encourage their children to take the lead in choosing activities. This approach fosters a sense of autonomy and self-discovery, empowering children to make decisions and explore their passions with confidence.

Encouraging children to take the lead in choosing activities doesn't imply a lack of guidance or structure. Purposeful parents provide a supportive framework within which children can explore their interests. This approach allows children to discover their strengths, preferences, and areas for growth, contributing to the development of a strong sense of self.

Promoting independence goes beyond extracurricular activities; purposeful parents encourage their children to take initiative in various aspects of their lives. Whether it's managing personal responsibilities, expressing opinions, or problem-solving, this encouragement fosters a spirit of independence that prepares children for the challenges and responsibilities of adulthood.

Conclusion

A balanced approach to nurturing children without overscheduling is essential for their overall development and well-being. Purposeful parents prioritize quality over quantity, allowing children the space and time for unstructured play, family bonding, and the pursuit of individual interests. By avoiding the pitfalls of overscheduling, parents create an environment that supports a child's physical, emotional, social, and intellectual growth. The ultimate goal is to raise well-rounded individuals who are not only academically proficient but also emotionally resilient, socially adept, and equipped with the essential life skills needed to navigate the challenges of the future.

*****